LA BELLA MAFIA

A single phrase from among the many memorable ones in this remarkable woman's gripping, powerful, so readable story nails it for me, and will do so for most readers: "…I learned how to cry." What a journey!
- Thomas B. Sawyer
Author of the bestselling thriller, *No Place to Run*,
Showrunner/Head Writer of *Murder, She Wrote*

This is one remarkable lady. She has a presence about her that just inspires you to want to reach out and help someone. We need more people out there like Bella Capo whose sole mission in life is helping women in serious need. Congratulations on a most definitely inspiring book and movement you have created.
- Ricky Cash and Aaron Phillips, Vegas Unwrapped Radio

Reading *La Bella Mafia* is like watching the movie Titanic. You know disaster looms, but the story is so compelling, you can't tear yourself away.
- Mike Dennis, Author of Man-Slaughter
http://mikedennisnoir.com

This story is riveting, somewhat painful to read, but imagine the Bella Capos of this world who weather this sort of physical and emotional abuse and come out on the other side willing to help others and educate the world! I cringed at the stories, the worded visuals, the turmoil this poor child and woman endured. What kind of strength that must take! Amazing recollection of a life nobody should have to experience.
- C. Hope Clark, Author The Carolina Slade Mystery Series
www.chopeclark.com
Editor, FundsforWriters, www.fundsforwriters.com
Writer's Digest 101 Best Websites for Writers, 2001-2013

It's great! "The most difficult books to read are often the books that are the most important to read. *La Bella Mafia* shows us the pain that exists all around us as well as those people who are struggling against it."
- John Brantingham, Author of Mann of War
Professor of English, Mt. San Antonio College

This book is the most heart-wrenching book I've ever read. It opens doors of understanding for those who have maybe not been through everything that this woman went through but perhaps parts of it. It also gives the reader an understanding as to why and how a person will allow themselves to be put through this Hell.

- Martha A. Cheves, Author, Reviewer

Shocking experiences of a little girl growing up in an incredibly dysfunctional family, then learning how to survive as an adult among others who are not what they seem. Unfortunately, far too common a reality that makes for an unforgettable read.

- Chris Roerden,
Author of Agatha Award winner *Don't Murder Your Mystery.*

The ultimate making lemons into lemonade story! Bella Capo's journey from horrific abuse to building La Bella Mafia, a worldwide network of women helping other women in trouble, will fill you with a sense of hope. An awe-inspiring story.

- Kris Neri, author of *Revenge on Route 66*
The Well Red Coyote bookstore

La Bella Mafia is a powerful, inspirational account of domestic violence and abuse and how one special woman dealt with the horrific mental and physical sequelae and the steps she is now taking to help those who suffer from this find a way out of their hell and back to a normal life. Bravo.

- Christie Tillery-French,
Award Winning Author/Poet, Dames of Dialogue blog

LA BELLA MAFIA

"I had endured so much, I was beyond feeling anything. Because I believe in angels, I had a crying angel tattooed on my back so it could cry for me when I couldn't cry for myself."
~Bella Capo

By
Morgan St. James
&
Dennis N. Griffin
As Told By
Bella Capo

LA BELLA MAFIA. Copyright © 2013 by Morgan St. James & Dennis N. Griffin.

All rights are reserved. Printed in the United States of America. No part of this book may be used or reproduced in any manner whatsoever without written permission except in the case of brief quotations embodied in critical articles and reviews. For information address Houdini Publishing, 6455 Dean Martin Dr. Suite L, Las Vegas, NV 89118.

ISBN: 978-1-936759-18-7

Cover design by Blake Whiteside
Printing Production Specialist- Barry Hess
Cover Photo by Mikel's Fine Art Photography
Edited by Judith Deutsch

Hair and Makeup for cover by La Bella Mafia Beauty, Las Vegas NV. 855-LA-MAFIA (526-2342)

www.houdinipublishing.com

DEDICATION

My biggest dedication is to God. Because of Him this book is a reality.

To my children, my grandchildren and my mother who have stood by me through all of the trials and tribulations.

To Tony "Nap" Napoli for standing by me with love and for holding my hand from one side of Hell to the other.

To Ali MacGraw, the best mentor a girl could have.

And, to Kathryn, my dear, dear friend from my earlier years.

ACKNOWLEDGEMENTS

In writing the acknowledgements for this book, there is no way I could possibly thank everyone who helped me survive, or those who saw me through the writing of La Bella Mafia. There are many human Angels out there and they know who they are. However, I will mention a few that come to mind.

My two aunts and two cousins, always dear to my heart.

Of course, Bella Nessy a very strong Prayer Warrior, the Bella Team and all of the individual Bellas who made this possible through their love and dedication to the cause and, in turn, make La Bella Mafia possible.

The Napoli siblings and sisters.

And my doctors, Dr. Dad and Dr. T, for their work and the care they have given me along with my therapist Mat, plus the amazing nurses who nursed me back to life more than once. They helped me find that will to live with the physical and emotional damage.

Doctor Robyn Westbrook, a very special woman.

My writers Morgan St. James, Dennis N. Griffin and editor Judy Deutsch for making this all happen. They are not just my writers, but have become my family and have helped me to organize my thoughts and words in a healing way as they held my hand through it all. It changed my life forever in a positive way.

My God daughter Marly and her mama—they are forever with me no matter where I go or what I do.

To Geoff, my best friend, who passed away from cancer a couple of years ago. He was a guardian angel for many years. Rest in peace.

Sonny and crew for being there through these last few years and the work they have done to help others who suffer from PTSD.

JR, the friend who walked me through the hardest two years while I got used to living away from the city. He talked me through my fears with a pure intended heart.

Gwynn and Linda, my two female friends and supporters who have held my hand in the new life that's been created, always there to help me and they have never thought of giving up.

Again, there is no way possible I could thank everyone but reading this, you know who you are. Thank you and God Bless each and everyone one of you.

Bella Capo

FOREWORD

I first met Bella about twenty-five years ago, in Malibu, California, where she was spending a period of time in a facility that purported to help young teenagers who were, for various, tragic reasons, caught between new foster homes and, often, Juvenile Hall. There were certain of us who went up there once a week to try to help these kids have some sense that people cared for them and wanted to try to make life a little easier. It was a very disturbing experience, as all of the boys and girls there had childhoods of indescribable fear and sorrow and neglect, as well as unspeakable abuse of every imaginable variety. This was my first experience realizing firsthand just how tragically many young people have negotiated that time which is supposed to be all about Innocence and Love. I was shocked and deeply saddened, and although I did go there every week for a long time, I never felt that there was much I could do…it was frankly devastating to witness.

Among the numbers of boys and girls I met, there were several who stood out, and none more so than a beautiful thirteen year old girl: This was Bella. At that time I had only a sketchy idea of the exact nature of the horrors she had survived, but it was clear that she had endured a level of abuse that was unspeakable and life changing. With all that, there was an enormous spark of Life to this particular child, and I remember thinking right away that Bella had an inordinate amount of resilience and a lack of self-pity that was amazing, given her history. Weekly, too, a group of well-meaning "art therapists" came to the facility to perhaps help unlock some of the children's pain through Art. Once, when we asked for whom a specific project was intended…as a special gift…I remember Bella saying, "my father," which stunned me, given the little I had learned of her home life. It was quite a revelation as to the deep, primal need kids have to reconstruct or remember their childhoods in an almost fairytale rewrite.

I spent a fair amount of time with Bella in particular, and grew to love her very special Spirit as well as her tough street-wise attitude. She was clearly a remarkable young woman, and I always thought that, given a chance, she would somehow work her way out of the darkness she had been forced to inhabit. Of course, I did not really know how that would come about, but I do remember thinking, "This one is a Survivor, and she is going to be Something." I saw her on and off for some years and watched her grow into the beautiful woman she is today, and along the way she married, and had a family of wonderful little girls. The last time I saw her she was in a lovely home with her family around her (including her exceptional mother, a survivor herself). I was thrilled to feel that she was happy at last, living with a man she loved and admired, and starting a brand-new life.

I will not spoil the extraordinary story you are about to read, except to say that her life took a surprising and terrifying turn several years ago, and the fact that this amazing woman…Bella…has turned her life into the inspiration it is now, is the reason for this book. Bella is a creature of pure Light, and in spite of another chapter of harrowing fear and darkness, she has triumphed over all of it and created a life that will be an inspiration to all who read about it. In addition to her four girls, she has added a huge blog where young women can go to be mentored by Bella and guided through some of the atrocities that she herself survived. Bella offers Hope and Solution and a Future to all of these women, and she is the embodiment not only of those qualities, but also of Love and Faith of the purest kind. She is one of the most remarkable people I have ever met, and I adore her and know that she will touch the heart of each and every one of you as you read and hear her story. You are in for a mind-blowing account of Courage and Forgiveness and Strength…and Love.

Ali MacGraw
Award-Winning Actress and Activist

PREFACE

On March 3, 2012, I received an email from Tony "Nap" Napoli, a highly-respected former associate of New York's Genovese organized crime family. His father was the late Jimmy "Nap" Napoli, who had been a boss with the Genovese family and at one time ran the largest illegal gambling operation in the United States.

I had first met Tony a few years earlier while doing research for one of my organized crime books. I found him to be extremely knowledgeable when it came to the history of the Mafia in America. He was also totally candid, except when it came to discussing current mobsters or their capers. In that regard, Tony is old-school and would rather rot in prison, himself, than compromise a former associate.

In this case, he asked me to help a friend of his who was looking for someone to assist her in writing a book. He said she had a great story to tell, but added that she had concerns for her safety. He would only identify her as Bella Capo. Could he give her my contact information?

Because I know Tony is the real deal, when he reaches out to me I always pay attention to what he has to say. And the mysterious Bella Capo increased my desire to learn more. I told Tony to have her contact me.

Shortly afterward, Bella Capo connected with me. As a result of numerous phone conversations and emails, I learned of the sexual, physical and emotional abuse she had suffered beginning at age four. This was followed by experimenting with street drugs, the onset of severe Post Traumatic

Stress Disorder (PTSD) and an ensuing addiction to prescription psychiatric medications. Knowing her experiences are shared by a multitude of women, Bella Capo probably would not have merited a book of her own. However, Bella Capo's story doesn't end there. This was just her beginning. What separates her story from the thousands of others like it is what happened afterward—she has survived, she has grown stronger, and she has reached out to succor other tortured souls. This, to me, makes Bella Capo's account an uplifting and compelling tale that must be told. I agreed to write it.

It was understood that security would be an issue, and that in most cases real names, and sometimes locations, could not be used. That eliminated the need for an Index, which I and some readers like to see in a nonfiction book. Thinking I had all of the bases covered, I started on the manuscript.

However, I soon realized that several of the subjects to be addressed were not my strong suits. For example, I was far from an expert on PTSD. And having been an only child, wasn't sure I'd be able to adequately address mother-daughter or sibling relationships. I decided to contact my friend and fellow author Morgan St. James, who had an encounter with PTSD following an automobile accident, is a mother and sibling, and who could provide further insight and understanding of Bella Capo's amazing life.

I ran the scenario past Morgan and she agreed with me that a book had potential. I'd never co-authored a book, but Morgan has a mystery series she wrote with her sister, and found the relationship workable. Bella Capo agreed to Morgan's participation and so began "Team Bella"—Bella Capo, Morgan, and me.

With more than one writer and three sets of fingers in the pie, Morgan suggested we bring in an outside editor to help catch typos, identify inconsistencies, and maintain continuity. This person would be able to tell if Morgan and I were melding our writing seamlessly, or if there were grammatical, stylistic, or literary distractions to the reader. Morgan recommended Judith Deutsch, who she had worked with in the past. Judy has a background in writing and editing and Morgan found her easy to work with. Bella Capo and I agreed, and Judy became Team Bella member number four. And what a great addition she is!

Another tremendous asset to the project was Tony Nap, who I mentioned earlier. Any time I needed information or clarification regarding an incident or situation he was involved in, he responded candidly and without hesitation. I didn't list him as a member of Team Bella, because Tony is unofficially known as the Godfather of La Bella Mafia for the guidance and support he offers.

Quite frankly, in the beginning stages I wasn't sure four people with different backgrounds living in various areas of the country—could work together efficiently to produce a well-written manuscript. But between conference calls, emails and the professionalism of my female colleagues on Team Bella, I believe we have done just that.

I hope that by the time you reach the end of La Bella Mafia, you will share our sense of awe and appreciation for what Bella Capo has accomplished against overwhelming odds.

Denny Griffin
Las Vegas, Nevada
April 10, 2013

PROLOGUE

I never believed I would be able to write about the shocking existence I endured from the time I was only four, but now I know I must if others are to be helped. Bella is not my given name, but it is who I have finally become and this is my story. My co-authors, Dennis Griffin and Morgan St. James, held my hand all the way through the trauma of reliving everything and have put my memories and stories into what you are about to read: La Bella Mafia.

I warn you, this book is not for the faint of heart. No child or young woman should ever have to go through what I did. If you looked at our family on the surface, we appeared to be living the American Dream with a nice house, luxuries, my father's successful career and plenty of his important friends. The dark secrets of a sadistically abusive father and brother, sexual abuse, ties to organized crime and free-flowing drugs should have had no place in the life of the little girl who twirled and danced in her perfect pink bedroom while wearing a fluffy tutu.

That lovely image was what everyone saw, while the horrendous underbelly of our family remained hidden, and continued into my life as a teen and an adult. You might think things like these only happen in movies, on TV or in fiction, but let me assure you, everything is true. By all odds, I should have died many times but something in me gave me the strength to close out the horrible reality, the physical abuse and living on the edge. Every page is stained with my tears.

I have been through hell on earth, but I know beauty like no other. My sole purpose is to keep reaching more people through the brutal honesty of my story.

There are many more like me, facing a life that makes them wish they were dead every day, but we are survivors.

We call ourselves La Bella Mafia.

****

Before I begin my story it is important that I tell you a few things about my family background; and specifically about my father—who and what he was—so you'll better understand what lurked beneath his successful public image and what my life was really like growing up.

I didn't have a very large extended family. My father had been adopted, so I had adoptive grandparents as well as grandparents and a couple of aunts and cousins on my mother's side, and that was it.

I remember staying with my adoptive grandparents during the summers when I was a little girl. My grandmother let me cook with her; and she did a lot of other stuff with me that I really enjoyed. When we slept out in her camper she let me sleep with her and I'd always kick her off the bed. Both of us thought that was funny. During those early years, staying with her was the closest I came to a normal life. I very seldom saw my maternal grandparents, but the few recollections I have of them are pleasant.

Childhood memories of my mother are scarce because the trauma of those years caused me to block most of them out. But there is one memory that is crystal clear: she was a drug addict. And that, I believe, was a contributing factor to some of the horrors I went through as a child.

Moving on to my father, he was born in February of 1951. He was a very large man, standing about 6'6" tall and weighing in the neighborhood of 250 pounds. He had dark skin and hair. I was forever in awe of how easily he did everything. For example, he loved motorcycles and built his very own Harley when he was around eighteen years old. And he built several more bikes after that. He was able to achieve almost anything if he set his mind to it.

As an adult he became involved in the production of semiconductors, and designed and built the plants where they are produced. After a plant was up and running he'd move to another area and build the next one. That meant my family never lived in any one place for very long.

Through his business activities he was able to bring a lot of people up the ladder of success with him. He built these men up out of nothing and made them into something. But my father was always the top dog, the leader, and those he helped elevate to become successful and respected businessmen were indebted to him. In my opinion it was like he was the leader of a kind of cult, and they were his followers.

He wanted to be the best and always took first place in everything he entered or tried. In addition to moving so often, we traveled from state-to-state showing off his bikes. Everywhere he went he constantly developed new contacts ranging from the biker gangs he was affiliated with, to lawyers, judges and politicians. His domineering personality coupled with his vast network of followers and connections, made him a very powerful overlord. He could make somebody's career with a phone call or a whispered word. And he could destroy them in the same way. Some of my father's personality and drive rubbed off on me and I am like him in some respects, in that I'm strong and can get people to follow my lead.

When I was still a child, our house was the scene of many parties and get-togethers. Virtually built for entertainment, one floor had a pool table, a handmade glass chess table, a fireplace and video games. Sometimes a hundred or more people were partying and other times just a handful of guys playing poker. But it was almost always busy, and marijuana was always available.

Despite my father's violent streak, he was my hero and I saw him as someone who could do anything and knew everyone. Back then I didn't question the "how" and "why" of it. I had no reason to. That's just the way it was.

Looking back, though, there were signs of how my father operated that I didn't pick up on. As a little child he took me into bars with him and I hid under the tables while he had meetings. I heard things, but at the time I was too young to understand. As I got older I'd hear him call people I knew he didn't like and have the friendliest conversations with them. It didn't seem important to me then, but now I realize he was gathering information about people that he could later use to coerce or intimidate them, and he also talked about tapping people's telephones. I guess the reason it didn't seem odd to me at the time was because I thought that's how things were done—to me it was normal.

Due to his connections, and the ability to get things done and make or break people, my father had the aura of a Mafia Godfather. People came to him for everything. And if he granted their request and helped them get what they wanted, then they owed him. People have asked me if he actually was in the Mafia. I don't know for sure either way. But I do know that he wielded Mafia-like power.

My father might have been a charmer, but he was also capable of extreme violence. He abused my mother physically and emotionally. And he physically abused both my brother and me.

On the following pages you'll learn much more about him, but I think that for now you know enough to be able to appreciate the world I lived in.

Bella Capo
April 15, 2013

PART ONE
My Hell on Earth

CHAPTER ONE

One of my earliest memories is of me as a little girl, all decked out in my ballerina outfit, my hair in pigtails. When I allow this memory to play in my head, it is as though I'm looking at a video of someone else. In my movie that little girl sits in a bedroom with pink walls and carpet. Even the bedroom furniture is designed to match the furniture in her doll house.

She plays with her dolls and her doll house, like any other little girl. But, if you think this is the picture of a happy child, you are dead wrong. Suddenly the "me" I view from a distance grabs a pair of scissors. She chops off her Barbie's hair, then makes the dolls beat and rape each other. Breathing heavily, she snatches up the mutilated dolls and throws them into a closet, pretending to lock the door. That's not what most little girls would have done with their beloved dolls, but she is acting out the things she sees every day—her normal.

Was she sending the abused dolls to a safe place by throwing them in the closet? I couldn't tell you, but I do know my closet was used as my own hiding place. I did weird stuff like hide food and other things in there. Years later I learned that abused children often hoard food and hide it in their rooms. Sometimes they eat as if there will be no more meals, even if they have no reason to feel insecure about their food supply. In fact, so much of my behavior was classic of abused children, even mutilating my poor Barbie dolls.

For example, I'd crawl up to the top floor and just sit in the closet. You see, there came a point when my tears stopped. From that time on, I couldn't feel anything. No wonder I can't stand to acknowledge that the child in my mental movie was me.

From the time I was four years old I lived for dancing. When I was dancing, I could be that perfect little girl in the perfect room with the perfect parents, not the "me" hiding in the closet who witnessed things so horrible they were squashed down in my memory for most of my life.

Dancing kept me going. Roller skating, the beach—these are the things that made me feel good. School was hard because I never could concentrate. I'd been thrown around and punched so much that my mind wasn't functioning right. But they didn't have traumatic brain injury awareness back then, so I just felt dumb and out-of-place.

My mom took me to dancing lessons three times a week, sewed outfits for my performances, got my hair done and was my biggest fan in the crowd. That part I do remember. But through the years I protected myself by suppressing so many memories, that it wasn't until a few years ago I had any memories of my mom at all. I just felt I had to protect her. I guess I'd just seen her battered or drugged-out so often I thought I could make it better.

Life at home was such a hell that I was suicidal from the time I was four years old. That was when I began to pray to Satan to take my life because I knew God wouldn't. I knew God wanted to save me, but being "me" was so hard.

Every time I'd done something wrong, I still felt I was a child of God, so I knelt down and cried with all my heart.

"Please, please God, forgive what I've done."

I experienced the comfort of Him telling me it was okay. He told me my life was going to be harder than most people's, but it would be okay. He told me to pray silently to Him because only He could hear my mind, and Satan couldn't.

That calmed me, but I couldn't grasp what it all meant and why I felt so different. Sure, there are times when everyone feels like they're different, but most four-year-olds don't think that way. They are still innocent, just past being toddlers. However, I knew who God was and believed what He told me—that I was here for a purpose. It wasn't a church that taught me I had to survive and have faith, either. It was something deep in my heart.

One memory I've recovered through therapy is the night my mom came home in the middle of the night and my father screamed at her so loudly that she gathered me up and took me to the spare room downstairs, where we hugged one another tightly, trying to shield each other from my father's wrath. But he blasted into the room with a huge jug of cold water and dumped it right over both of us. As the vision of that awful night flashed into my mind, I shivered just as though the water was hitting me again and desperately tried to cling to the rare happy memories I have instead, like her getting me ready for a dancing recital.

When I got old enough to go to school, I pulled Cs even though I wasn't trying. By the third grade I'd quit going home after school and went to my friend Heidi's house instead.

That's where I experienced my first molestation outside of my own family. For a long time I didn't tell anybody. It was disgusting. She gave her older brother blowjobs and did all kinds of other sexual things. He threatened to tell and then pulled out the porn magazines and made us mimic the photos. He and my own brother were two-of-a-kind and they wielded a crazy power over us by making us believe we were the ones who were wrong.

I was terrified of what would happen to me and to Heidi if my parents found out, instead of being confident they would support me and the boy would be punished. It may be hard for someone who hasn't walked in my shoes to understand. And you may even think I plead my case too vigorously, but I went by what I saw happening to my own mother. How could I know that wasn't the way it was supposed to be?

Finally, I couldn't take it anymore, and I did tell my family what was happening. Who do you think was the most pissed? It was my brother, who was abusing me, too. Why do you suppose he was upset? Because he didn't have control over these episodes with Heidi's brother.

The police got involved but no arrests were made. Heidi's family moved away very suddenly. Looking back as an adult, I don't think it was a coincidence. My father would have used his power, connections and influence to achieve this outcome. As for the police department's disinterest, it only reinforced in my little-girl head that people like my father could do whatever they wanted. He was able to resolve problems in his own way.

The San Diego neighborhood I grew up in was close. On the surface it looked like the American Dream with nice houses and cars in a well-tended atmosphere. We all played kick-the-can and other childhood games.

But there was a big, dark, secret among us all and that was the little sexual underworld of molestations that occurred from one house to another.

My best friend, Kelli, was older than my brother. She also was the only one who stood up to my father and hid me in her house when things got really bad. It took a lot of courage because as I said, everyone was afraid of my father, and that was a fact.

A few years ago I reconnected with one of Kelli's brothers on Facebook, and the first question he asked was, "So did he (my brother) grow up to run gangs like your father?"

I laughed to myself and replied, "No, the little girl in the tutu did."

CHAPTER TWO

Showing your rapes to the world isn't an easy thing to do, but I knew years ago I had to when the time was right.

When your reality is a living Hell, you actually do believe you did something wrong and that's why you're there. The first time I sat in a therapist's chair I didn't feel like I deserved to be there. Of course, I have come leaps and bounds from that time and now I pour out my soul every day in the hope my message will reach even one girl who feels the way I did. If that happens, it will spare her some of the torment of finding her way. That's how La Bella Mafia began. Most of the Bellas are women I touched who had experienced what I did and worse. We've bonded to help each other. It is never really over, but it can get better.

Sometimes men are surprised to learn women are really delicate and strong at the same time. Women aren't the only ones abused, either. My heart is as big as Texas and I've come to realize that it's a blessing and a curse. Everything I say here is the truth. I'm a pushy person, though, and I've been told by so many people who know me that I'm a miracle—because I survived when I could have died so many times.

I have told myself I only have to write the book once. After that I'll only have to open it to autograph it. By committing this work to paper, I hope to release some of the memories from my mind and find a better peace.

I can still close my eyes and see this scene clearly—the turning point where my brother's torments changed into forced adult sexual activity and perversion for me.

He and his friend had pinned a neighborhood girl down on a trampoline in the latter's backyard. She was older than them, but I'd heard my parents say she was "retarded." At that time I didn't really know what the word meant. All I knew was she acted like a little kid even though she was bigger than they were.

My brother held her hands down and his friend tugged at her panties. She screamed, but my brother and his friend were too strong for the girl. I wanted to do something to help her, but they were so much bigger than me. I thought maybe I could run at them and hit them, but what good could a four-year-old do against two husky eight-year-olds? They would just brush me off like a bothersome fly, and I was so afraid of my brother.

His voice broke through my thoughts.

"Hey, look at that." He pointed to the girl who was still screaming. "The retard's bleedin' all over the place."

They had succeeded in pulling down her pants and were frowning at what looked like a big wad of cotton. It was covered with blood and I really got scared. What had they done to her? I had no idea what a period was. All I knew was that they had done something awful to that girl. Her eyes were alive with terror and she was bleeding onto the trampoline.

I was so scared I could hardly find my voice, but at last began to shout as loud as I could, "Stop doing that to her! Stop it! Let her go!"

My brother laughed. "Whadda ya think? That you

can stop us?" Suddenly his face changed. "Hey, what if the brat tells on us?" He leered at me with smoldering hatred. Then he turned to the girl, "Pull up your pants and get out of here. You can understand that, can't you, Dummy? Get the hell out of here."

The girl shot me a look and I still remember the gratitude in her eyes. In a clumsy motion she put herself back together and lumbered off.

My brother's voice turned hard and flat. "Okay, wiseass. We're still gonna do stuff, but now that the retard is gone, who's left?" He grabbed me and threw me down on the trampoline. "You!"

It was no challenge for those two boys to pin me down and play out their fantasies. I fought, but I was too weak against them.

The next thing I heard was my brother shouting, "Open your mouth. My friend is going to do stuff to you like they do in Dad's movies. If you tell anyone, I'll beat the hell out of you. Open it! Now!"

With the girl gone, I'd taken her place. By saving her I'd condemned myself and it was never the same for me again. That was the day I really became my brother's sex toy.

Tears leaked from the corners of my eyes before they turned into a downpour. Maybe the tears got to him, I don't know, but when my brother saw how hard I was crying he finally said, "That's enough. We don't want the brat crying like that or blabbing about what we did."

In a heartbeat I'd entered the world of adults in the worst way possible, forced to submit because I was so afraid of being beaten up.

As I look back at that incident now, I know there comes a time in your life when you have to stop accepting the role, to stop allowing yourself to be victimized. I was way too young to defend myself back then, so my brother did whatever he felt like with me, playing on my fear of him. It went on—and on, getting worse by the year. Some of my stories will shock you to the core, but the monsters have to come out of the closet. These things do happen in some families in real life.

Even when you learn to fight back, does it mean dangerous people will just vanish and all the hurt will stop? Absolutely not! But what it does mean is that you are willing to get enough education to take the power back into your own hands rather than allowing these "fiends" to be as gigantic as they are when, truly, they're just scumbags. When you can do that, you'll know who holds the power—you!

It's not magic. You'll still get hurt, you'll still cry, but you'll be able to kick-ass and not allow these knuckleheads to take such control. That all sounds good, but it's easier said than done. Trust me, I know.

CHAPTER THREE

My brother did a lot of bad stuff, and sometimes I marvel at the fact that he never got caught. But my dad was gone so much and my mom was out of it on drugs most of the time, so I guess he had the freedom to do pretty much anything his twisted mind could conceive.

We got our first big screen TV way before most people had one, so whenever my brother invited his friends over, they immediately got into my dad's porn collection. I kept trying to convince myself that between the abuse, visual education from watching so many porn films and his anger, maybe my brother was trying to show me love the only way he knew how. But looking back as an adult, I realize that was much more a wish on my part than a reality. It was no such thing.

He'd get his friends high with no limit on how much of my dad's weed they smoked. When they were high and horny from watching the porn, it was time for them to use me for their fun. Sometimes he locked me in a room with them, but sometimes we never even made it to the room.

One time he actually laid me down in the hallway. In my mind's eye all I can see is a blur of faces. He had our pet

Doberman perform sexual acts on me while they watched, and I just laid on the floor, crying.

Make no mistake. Making me submit to things like that wasn't a one-time circus act. It became a regular attraction. By that time it didn't matter to me anymore. I was past feeling or caring. I know now the only thing that saved me is that I was never completely penetrated during any of the sexual acts they made me do. My brother did manage to penetrate me partly, but never got all the way in. That part was left to their tongues. Technically I was still a virgin, at least physically.

Between the beatings and the mind-fucking, it's no wonder I lived in fear of him and did whatever he commanded me to without protesting. As all of these forbidden memories bubble to the surface now it's hard to accept he was only four years older than me, and yet wielded such power. He was truly his father's son.

Now add the craziness my dad brought into the house. The feelings and thoughts I perceived as normal actually signaled the early beginning of post traumatic stress disorder, or PTSD as it's known.

I later learned that due to the PTSD, I disassociated. I didn't fight. I didn't get violent, and I didn't yell. I internalized everything and that's where all the suicidal tendencies came from.

I always beat the crap out of myself for doing one little thing wrong. My father conditioned me to be like that the entire time I was growing up. For example, my toy box was the neatest little kid's toy box you've ever seen. But obsessive neat freak that he was, it wasn't unusual for my father to storm into my room, and yell like a crazy person that I had to empty my toy box and rearrange it or else. His demands included things like making me dust off his motorcycle trophies with Q-Tips. How nuts was that? Q-Tips? As soon as my brother and I heard his car in the driveway, terror always kicked in and we jumped up and acted like we'd spent the whole day cleaning.

He had this cupboard filled with food and if anyone touched it they would get beaten severely. I'd never really suffered the beatings when I was young, but my brother did. I knew that whenever my brother got beaten by my dad, I was going to be beaten by my brother next. Period! So what was the difference? In the end we were both battered.

That man, my father, broke my heart so many times I stopped counting. All I wanted was to have him be the hero I thought he was. The more I have learned and talked about it through therapy and pouring my heart out here, the more I know he was anything but a hero.

I endured so much from my earliest years that I developed an innate, even clever ability to come up with ways to survive or to get retribution.

When I was eleven we lived in Fremont in Northern California, for what I call a brief moment. I was at the stage where my rebellion had started to really develop, and I hated myself but never knew why.

One day a girl at school heard me say I didn't want to live. She taunted me and made fun of me and it didn't stop there. She enlisted others to participate in her attacks on me.

In my head I decided to make her pay. I am not a violent person, but rather a very psychological one. The first thing I did was to befriend her and get close to her.

The day came when we cut school and went to her house for some drinks and partying. What she didn't know was that I'd planned for this and had a tube of Super Glue with me. While she was doing other things, I Super Glued everything I could think of. The phone to the hook, the VCR shut, vases to the table—when I was done, nothing moved.

Within a day, my parents got a call from the authorities that the family whose stuff I had Super Glued had filed a complaint and I was going to be sent to Juvenile Hall. "Well,"

I thought, "not if I can help it!" So, out my window I went and was gone for two weeks.

What a two weeks it was! I met up with some strangers I thought were high school kids and stayed with them. They had me partying, smoking a ton of weed and drinking. One guy did try to have sex with me, but, since I had never been penetrated by a male penis, in my eyes I was still a virgin and I wanted to keep it that way, at least for awhile. Sex wasn't something that was "fun" for me and it was something I could certainly live without.

One night we went driving up a canyon and played games with the car lights off, but something went wrong and we went off the side of the road. I remember that it was a long drop, but I don't even recall feeling afraid. Just numb. I could have died in that crash, but luckily we landed on some trees that were hanging out of the side of the canyon wall. It was nothing short of a miracle. We crawled out, made our way back up to the road and I walked to a friend's house rather than going home.

My parents were looking for me, and they paid off one of my friends who knew where I was to rat on me. My mom came to get me and when I saw her crying, I went with her without a fight. I came home to a house full of detectives in suits who were waiting for me. They didn't want to talk with me about Super Glue. That incident had seemingly been dropped. Their questions were about something much more serious: murder.

Apparently these kids I had been hanging out with the prior two weeks, the ones I just thought were high schoolers, had killed a foreign exchange student. They robbed her of $500, stabbed her to death and dropped her body off in the river down the street from my house. To show how out of touch with reality I was by then, although it kind of startled me, it didn't bother me very much. It did make me sad for the girl and mad at the guys that did it, but no real fear for my own safety. You see, I knew all too well what it was to live on the edge, even at that age. I'd had to shut off all of my feelings just to survive each day. Death was just one more thing that was normal in my vision of reality.

As time went on my brother continued inflicting extreme sexual and physical abuse on me and other neighborhood kids, too. Nothing was off-limits, including sexual acts with animals. I never told anyone because of his threats and how severely he beat me.

So there was no brotherly love. Instead, I developed brotherly hate. I can look at it now and realize that my father abused my mother and brother, and my brother took it out on me. As for my mother, her escape was drugs. One night she asked me to roll a joint for her so I did. Then I broke it in two and gave her half. She got mad and made me give her the other half, too.

All I could think was, "Well, why ask if you're not going to share, right? Don't ask your kid if it's only for you." So I ran away again. Running away became another one of my norms.

I remember my father came home from work one day and got into a terrible fight with my mother. I can still see him kicking her down the stairs into our sunken living room. But he didn't touch me. At this point he was very sensitive to me. Everyone else got beatings from him, but he still thought of me as that little girl with the perfect pink bedroom who twirled in her tutu and I was safe from him, at least for the time being.

That wasn't the case for my brother, though. My father would wake him up out of a deep sleep and tear his bedroom apart. When my brother was only eight, my father thought nothing of throwing him against the wall and bloodying his nose for doing something as minor and stupid as using my father's hairbrush.

It seemed like there was always violence. I can remember one night when my brother and I were at a shelter for abused kids. That's where we went when things were too rough. My mom showed up in the middle of the night, frantic that my father was trying to kill us and told them we had to leave.

It was believable to the people at the home, and they packed us up. You know how you remember weird things, sort of like the things you picture in a dream? Well, this wasn't a dream. There I was, wearing my mom's pants which were many sizes too big for me. My mom was in a psychotic episode from speed and drove up the off-ramp and onto the freeway against traffic.

Soon there was a bunch of cops behind us trying to get her to pull over. But she kept on going, screaming that my father was going to kill us. She finally stopped and they dragged her out of the car. She was so high and so out of it, that it took many cops and a head banging to get her on the ground for cuffing.

I sat in the front seat with my brother watching as mom kept fighting and screaming, and then managed to get out of the cuffs somehow. At that point I peed my pants.

When my mother was released from the police station, my father kicked her down the stairs and I ran away, again, to escape the violence. The next day I went to school and told the counselor what had happened. The authorities put me into a shelter. Shortly after that, my mom went into rehab.

CHAPTER FOUR

Before my mother went into rehab she was so messed up on drugs she had lost touch with reality. You would think that would make me afraid of drugs, but I went exactly the other way, getting my first high when I was only eleven. What I thought I would never forgive her for was finding an escape for herself, but leaving me unprotected from my father's and brother's abuse. I find that to be an even greater crime than the abuse itself. I've since forgiven her for that failing. But it took many years and lots of praying before I was able to let it go.

If there's one topic I tend to dance around, it's my father. I suppose learning he wasn't the hero I looked up to, but a man who could be evil, was my most painful realization.

Shortly after my mom went into rehab in Southern California, I got out of foster care and went back to living with my father in Northern California. It wasn't long before I knew I had lost my father as well.

One day, a family friend who owned a Harley shop came over to visit my father. My dad was working on something in the garage, so I answered the door, happy to see this man I had known all my life as "Uncle Rick." I smiled at him having no hint of what was coming next.

Uncle Rick reached out and pinched my little eleven-year-old boobies and then took one hand and put it between my legs all the while telling me how much I had grown up. I was in complete shock. This was not somebody I would have expected something like this from.

I ran into the kitchen crying and called my mother at rehab to tell her what had just happened. I don't know why I was driven to tell her, because now that I think about it, I never told anyone about all of the other abuse. Maybe I was able to get up the nerve to tell her because this happened when it was just Dad and me living in the house. My brother finally couldn't take my dad's beatings anymore and had gotten himself into a foster home. So, I guess I felt safe with my brother gone.

Well, my mom called the police and in no time they came to the house, swept me up and took a report. A restraining order was immediately put on Uncle Rick that turned out to be nothing more than a joke. Telling my mom resulted in my first real beating by my father and he let Uncle Rick come back to the house the very next day.

I think it was at this point I decided the world was a cruel place and I was going to go my own way. With my mother and brother gone and my father an alcoholic, I was now raising myself. Still a pre-teen, I was literally on my own.

That was when I started my first gang, The Diamond Girls, and filled my days with cutting school, taking LSD and bringing my own friends home to smoke some of the marijuana my dad kept in a big baggie up in the liquor cabinet.

I was in the sixth grade by then and one day when I was high on LSD I tried to give a report from a blank sheet of paper. That was when I knew it was time to give up on school, and rarely went again until I was placed in a foster home. It was mind-boggling to me that I was never caught and the school system continued to pass me all the way through the

10th grade.

I had always been so lost and isolated in my own little world that I'd never felt like I was really a part of anything. After I put the Diamond Girls together, we had what I looked at as a lot of good times. I wasn't interested in boys, and sex was the last thing I was eager to get into. Having friends and partying—being able to laugh—was new to me.

To my amazement, some of The Diamond Girls even stood up to my father when I ran away again—amazing because in the past, other than Kelli, nobody ever stood up to him. They were all afraid of his physical size and power.

By then, my father was having an affair with a woman half his age. Worse yet, she was soon to be my stepmother. If you close your eyes and picture the prime example of a blonde bimbo, that was her.

For some reason she felt it necessary to tell me her problems. She said she was a nurse and had a lot of patients who had died, so she left nursing and went into the business where my father worked. She did some sort of corporate sales.

A little kid didn't need to know the kind of stuff she told me. The three of us might be on something as innocent as a hike, when all of a sudden this bimbo whispered stupid things to me, like she wasn't wearing underwear. Why in the world would I want to know that?

I really didn't like her. Looking back, she was basically just a kid who was screwing my dad. Now with my mom in rehab, she was practically screwing him in my face. One night she screamed so loud during their sex I had to yell at her to shut up so I could get some sleep. There were times we tried to "fake like" each other, but that's all it was—fake, just like her.

Eventually my father changed companies and we moved to Oregon and into a huge house. It was a lovely place with a creek running through the backyard. The bimbo didn't move with us, and that was good. But when my father flew out-of-state or out of the country on business, he left me there all alone with no one to watch out for me.

In the beginning I tried to go to school a few times, but I definitely didn't fit in. I became friends with Jill, the girl next door, and after that never went to school. I stayed home and she did, too. We drank my father's Smirnoff, 190 proof Everclear, orange juice, wine—you name it and we drank it. I also started inhaling Super Glue. The girls in the gang had taught me to do that, so now I had another way of shutting down. My behavior was totally self-destructive, but I really had no interest in living and didn't see a future, so why try? If only I'd had somebody there to guide me or support me.

Later on Dad's girlfriend joined us for a short time, but she couldn't take it and moved back to California. Trying to understand their relationship and my part in it was always confusing to me.

It was around that time that severe beatings from my father began on a regular basis.

CHAPTER FIVE

When my father was away on one of his business trips and I was supposed to be getting ready to visit my mom in rehab, I decided to throw a big party for all the neighborhood kids before I left. After all, there was no one there to say I couldn't.

Sure, some might think I was a spoiled rich brat taking advantage of having a house to myself with no parent around. Kids don't think like adults. Throwing this party for my friends seemed like a cool thing to do, but at the same time I might have been taking out some anger at always being left to fend for myself. Who knows what I expected when I scheduled that party, but it turned into something that took on a life of its own and got totally out of control. There was sex going on in my upstairs bedroom. Even worse, some of the people at the party had sex in my father's huge bedroom just down the hall from mine and left signs of cocaine in his bed.

If that wasn't bad enough, somebody took sex pictures with my dad's camera and then couldn't get the film out. Things were thrown out the windows and butter was stuffed into the exhaust pipes of people's cars. One boy and girl wanted to have sex and wanted me to have sex with this guy who was supposed to be my boyfriend after they were finished. I agreed and they went into the room and did their thing. But when it came to my turn, I just laughed in their faces and said, "Like you thought I really would do that?"

As I said, it got really wild, beyond anything I could have imagined. I went along with the flow, and allowed these supposed friends to run rampant, stupidly believing my father wouldn't find out about it. If I'd been more mature, I would have realized the evidence was there for him to see, and it would cost me dearly.

When he found out about the party, I endured the beating of my life. I'd been naive enough to think I had already experienced my father's worst rage. As often happens with PTSD, I have no memory of what happened first, but I do remember that we were upstairs and he was drunk. He suddenly picked me up by my hair, called me a slut, and kicked me all over my body with his steel-toed boots. Then he tossed me from room-to-room by my hair, kicking me all the while.

I remember flying through the air as though I weighed nothing. He'd drop me hard and pick me up again, throw me in the air once more and when I landed, slam me with full-blown punches to my face.

Finally, he threw me from my room into my bathroom and I landed hard in the bathtub. I tried to shrink away from him as he came back at me, but he pulled me by my hair again and kicked me down the winding stairs that led to the first floor. I bounced like one of those lightweight bouncy balls and landed in a crumpled heap at the bottom of the steps.

Not done yet, he picked up my square, hard suitcase—the one that was packed for my trip to see my mom—and hurled it at my head. It caught me full-on. Not only was my body broken, so was my heart. How could the daddy I loved so much do this to me? At that moment my love-hate relationship with my father began. Although I would continue to despise him for what he did to me, he remained the person whose approval I sought above all others.

But the violence of that day wasn't quite over. By now his face had turned beet red. He snatched up the phone and called my mom in California. Somewhere in my head, through all of the pain, I heard him scream into the phone, "You better talk to your daughter because I'm beating the shit out of her." Then he shoved the receiver into my hand.

Mom's voice was shaking but firm as she said, "Do whatever you need to, but get to me."

Well, I was supposed to go to California the next day, anyway. While my mom kept telling me to get out, he was continuing to drink. When I hung up, he yelled at me to go clean the kitchen spotless. He followed me into the kitchen and pulled his foot back to kick me again.

Even though my body was beyond feeling pain by then, I just knew I couldn't take another hit, another kick. I picked up a knife from the counter and whispered to myself, "One more time mother-fucker—just one more time."

He didn't deliver the kick. Instead he staggered off and passed out on the couch. I know now that I was wrong for having the party. But at eleven and raising myself, I was making my own decisions. And many of them were bad.

The next morning I got ready to go to the airport and covered up as many of the facial and body bruises from the beating as I could.

My father stood by the car and shouted, "Give me the key to the house!" His face was like stone. I stood there frozen with my heart racing because I had lost the key. An image popped into my head. I did have another silver key that looked similar. Maybe he would think that was the right one, so I took a chance and gave it to him. Then I prayed. Thank goodness he didn't try it in the door.

While we were in the car driving to the airport, out of nowhere he punched me in the face with his closed fist and shouted, "I hate you and I never want to see you again." And then he put $500 in my pocket. To him, money could fix anything. He must have thought it would take away the physical and emotional trauma he'd inflicted on me.

My mom's rehab facility in Pasadena, California, had given permission for me to stay for a while. When I got there I saw my mom sober for the first time in my memory. What she saw was a bunch of bruises all over her daughter. She put me in the car and took me to the police station. They stripped me and took pictures from head to toe. I really didn't need that.

When they finished taking the photos, my mother told me my father would be punished for what he'd done and I'd never have to go back to him. I'm sure she was sincere when she said that and I believed her. But things don't always work out the way we hope.

CHAPTER SIX

With the signs of the beating he had given me all over my body, my father was charged with child abuse. That was where it ended, though. The case never went to trial or mediation. He claimed that my injuries were the result of a fight I'd gotten into at school and they believed him. Forget that there was no record of a fight at the school I rarely went to. He'd come out on top again.

After the court dropped the charges, he tried to bribe me with money and dance school in France if only I would come home. But my broken body was simply too tired to endure his temper. My mother had said I wouldn't have to go back, and I begged to go to a foster home instead.

They flew me back to Northern California where I was placed in a shelter, but fortunately didn't have to stay in that institutional setting for very long. I put myself in the hands of Social Services, and reasoned that anything would be better than the life I had known for my previous eleven years.

The thought of going into my first real foster home was weird. Making a decision like that is a desperate thing for a kid to do—leaving what they know for the unknown—

but who wouldn't want to get away from beatings and abuse? I guess I was the poster child for "desperate," and my case worker recognized that.

Alone and empty, traveling to that new home with no idea what was going to happen next, all I knew was that I couldn't take it anymore at my father's house and I'd done the only thing I could to get out. With my brother gone and Mom living in rehab without any place for me to stay, I was on my own. No longer able to handle emotions, I finally shut down for the most part. There was one emotion I never lost, however, and that is the ability to love. I'd sit there staring at a wall or the ceiling and ask myself, "Why can I still feel love?" The only explanation that made any sense to me is God is love.

I never expected to fall in love with my first foster mom. How blessed I was to have her. Connie was an African-American woman who lived down the street from my school. This wonderful woman was about five-foot-five, dark skinned and she wore her hair in a bun. Her friendly smile lit up a room and every now and then she snuck in a hug.

Not only that, but I really appreciated the way she respected my boundaries. Connie never pushed herself on me, never showed me disrespect and gave me the healthy unconditional love I craved. I finally went back to the school I should have been attending all along. There were other foster kids in Connie's home, and we were like a rainbow—a little Mexican brother and sister, two little black girls and a young white boy who followed me around like I was the coolest thing in the world.

Robert was dorky, but I liked having him around sometimes. I learned there was a big difference between an abusive big brother and an annoying little brother. We took walks through the streams and smoked cigarettes. He went to the same school and always wanted to be seen with me. I'd lie in bed at night, snuggle under my blankets and think, "So this is what a real normal family is like." Then I'd try to figure out if the "normal" I'd known all my life could have been love by any stretch of the imagination.

Connie was amazing. I threw big temper tantrums filled with the anger I'd held inside for so long. When she asked me, "What's wrong?" I stomped off and shouted back, "Nothing." She mimicked what I was doing to show me what I looked like, but instead of continuing to rub it in, she left chocolate chip cookies out in the middle of the night to let me feel like I'd sneaked one. She knew what she was doing. Those simple things gave me a sense of the little girl who still lived somewhere inside me—I just didn't know where.

During the days when I was in school or with my old gang, The Diamond Girls, she cleaned the kids' rooms. I think she understood that my childhood had been stolen, and didn't get on me for smoking cigarettes. In fact, after she made my bed, she put the cigarettes right back between the mattress and box spring where she'd found them. I was always grateful she didn't look in the piggy bank, though, because that's where I kept my acid.

I used acid from the time I was eleven until I was twelve-and-a-half. I loved the feeling of laughing uncontrollably, walking around the block for hours and hours letting the time just fly by. I'd lived in fear for so long that I'd never known what it was to just laugh from the gut with a never-ending smile. It's sad that I had to use something like that to accomplish a feeling that is normal for most kids, but it was what it was.

Never once during the nine months I was with Connie did I want to talk to my father. I couldn't forgive him for what he had done to me. On my twelfth birthday he sent a big gorilla with a huge bouquet of balloons. Although he's been dead for quite some time now, as unbelievable as this sounds, there is still a strange connection between us and balloons. It is actually a little surreal. They come to me in the oddest places and at the oddest times. It is as though he's letting me know he's there and desperately trying to reconnect.

Some of my roommates and my ex-husband have actually been freaked out by a balloon following them through the house. I never try to capture or hold the balloons, but their presence does touch my heart. Who knows if he's still out there somewhere?

While my mom was in rehab, she took all the parenting classes that were necessary and went above and beyond what it took to repair the damage of my dysfunctional childhood and build the relationship I had always wanted. My father, on the other hand, had only one person he cared about outside himself, my future step-mother, and that was it.

I was so happy living with Connie! For the first time I had a real home life with the feeling of a family gathered around watching a TV show and eating dinner together. And then it ended. My father petitioned the Family Court to have me returned to him. With no input from me, a judge granted my father's request. The thought of leaving Connie's and going back to an environment that lacked love and one where beatings were a certainty, was terrifying. I couldn't let it happen! After resisting and fighting with everything I had, the law won and away I went.

So when I went back to my father's house it was because I had no choice, but it didn't last long. He gave me everything money could buy, but money wasn't enough. There was no way it could replace Connie's love and her fresh, hot cookies. Life has always had a deeper meaning to me than what money can buy. I craved real love. Funny, I can envision the bimbo who would become my stepmother taking me shopping for school clothes during that time and yelling at me because I didn't want anything but black. Well, screw her! Black gave me a sense of power and allowed me to hide in a crowd when I wanted to. My clothing was one of the few things I had a choice in. Not much has changed in that department. I still wear lots of black.

As for the future step-monster, I never respected her. Why would I? She surely didn't respect me. In fact she constantly lambasted me with all of the jealous, cruel things she felt in her head. Between his obsession with her and work, my father was so consumed that money was the only thing he had left to offer me. I'd rather live on the streets if living in a million-dollar house like ours meant constant fighting and being deprived of the real love that I had briefly experienced.

Very quickly things got so bad at my father's house that I pleaded with my social worker to help me. This time I couldn't go back to Connie because that bed had been filled and there was no room for me, so I was placed in the main shelter for kids. Instead of the warm, loving home I looked forward to, the shelter was like a basketball coliseum, sectioned off with beds and a room to eat and a room for doctor's appointments. It was a locked facility, and they controlled everything every kid did. I imagined it was probably very much like living in Juvenile Hall, except that my only crime was being unable to tolerate beatings. Why was I there?

I became what they called a "leaver." If there was a way to get out, something that wasn't locked, I'd find it and vanish. I spent periods of time living on the streets, but they always found me and sent me back. Sometimes I'd find my way to Connie's house and pour my heart out to her.

Finally, Connie talked her cousin into letting me stay with her. Bernice was a big woman who really wasn't interested in giving me a home. She had simply agreed as a favor to her cousin. She lived in a one-bedroom apartment, so I slept in the bed and she slept on the couch. I'm sure she resented having to give up her bed to me. I wasn't an easy kid to manage, always on the run and out for fun. I met some teenagers in the apartment building and found I could "escape" through the bedroom window to get together with them.

While I was with Bernice my period started. Except

for the time my brother and his friend held that poor neighborhood girl down on the trampoline when I was four, I knew nothing about what a period was other than the whispers of my friends. When I woke up one morning there was brown on my sheets. I didn't know what it was, and up to that time I never had the relationship with my mother where she would have given me the talk all mothers have with their daughters. And although my father's girlfriend never hesitated to tell me all about her sexual escapades, she never told me the important things a young girl needed to know.

So, full of embarrassment, I hid the sheets and got dressed for school. During class my pants felt damp and sticky. When I looked, there were red stains coming through my white pants. This time I knew it was blood and I was scared to death. What horrible thing had happened to me? Why was I bleeding? The teacher sent me to the nurse's room and she explained to me about periods and gave me some pads.

The beginning of the end with Bernice was rapidly approaching. During a party some of my apartment house friends threw, I took the only beer in Bernice's fridge and managed to sneak out the bedroom window. Beer didn't hold the thrills of drugs I'd taken in the past, but the adrenalin that pumps when you get away with something becomes like a drug. I was hooked on that, but didn't know it.

I'd established a bit of a reputation, and a girl at the party asked me if I could get some cocaine. Well, I didn't use cocaine or know where to get it, but I couldn't risk my reputation now that I had one, so I went back through my window and got some aspirin out of the medicine cabinet. I crushed it up finely while I tried to picture what coke looked like. I took the crushed aspirin back to the party and watched as the girl snorted it. She looked at me afterwards and thanked me. I tried to hold in the laughter when she said, "That was some really good stuff."

The party didn't last long and neither did my stay with Bernice. Taking the beer was the last straw. She decided I couldn't stay there any longer and back to the shelter I went.

This time I wanted to be closer to my mother, so I talked it over with my case worker. He was a very nice man with short hair and a well-trimmed beard, probably 5'8" or so. He always dressed in jeans and had a very casual air about everything, so he put me at ease. I never felt like he was a threat. We often drank lemonade together and he played a big role in keeping me on track. He told me about his family and made me feel like he genuinely cared what happened to me. Finally, he found a rehab center in Malibu that would be close to my mom, and took the airplane to Southern California with me.

That was the beginning of another life. Team House would be my home for the next nine months.

CHAPTER SEVEN

Team House! When I think back to my stay there the image that comes to mind is a cult. No joke. That wasn't my first impression, though—far from it.

I remember the day my social worker and I boarded the plane in San Jose, California, for the trip to Los Angeles. The sun was shining brightly and I was really upbeat. I was going back to Southern California—my favorite place—and what I hoped would be a stable and long-lasting place to live. We drove along the ocean on Pacific Coast Highway from Los Angeles to Malibu. The view was fantastic, with all the beautiful sandy beaches and the seemingly endless waves.

After turning off the highway, we drove up a winding tree-lined road and then down another street to a long gravel driveway that led to the privately owned Team House complex. There was a large main building with a smaller building behind it that was used as a school. In addition to the main house, there was also a storage building and several houses that could hold between twelve and twenty kids, depending on the number of rooms used for bedrooms and the number of kids assigned to each. People donated all sorts of things, but the kids did all the cooking and shopping as though we were really being trained to be part of society. We all had chores, and each group had their own house—the place where they lived like a family. Various staff members came in and out to help us with shopping, cooking and other things, and there was one main counselor for each house. Other staff members gave us our lessons.

On the surface it appeared to be an excellent rehabilitation facility with the purest of motives.

After a few days, one of the kids told me this area of Malibu, above Zuma Beach, was not very far from Johnny Carson's house. Like I said, on the surface everything appeared so perfect—nothing at all like the awful place Social Services put me in before I went to Bernice's. Most of the counselors, teachers and clerical people gave the appearance of being very professional.

My first few hours at Team House, I felt pretty happy about how things were turning out. I gave my social worker a big hug as we said "goodbye" and I watched him drive away. Neither of us had a clue as to what I'd just gotten into.

I was assigned to a house with ten boys and girls of various ages, the majority of whom were white. Their ages ranged all the way from about twelve to eighteen years old, so I was one of the youngest. After settling in, it was time for me to get oriented.

For the next several days I just sat around observing the other kids and learning the ropes. The rules were strict, like no smoking, no caffeine, no candy bars, no sodas, and if you broke the rules you had to confess to it in what they called "Circle." I will talk more about that a little later. Circle was like going to confession in church and asking to be forgiven for something that most kids would consider normal. I sensed from my fellow residents that you'd better think twice before you broke any of those rules.

During the day we sometimes went shopping for groceries and clothes. Because we weren't conditioned to feel guilt yet, a staff member supervised us. When we advanced to admission of guilt for breaking rules, we could go with a partner instead of a supervisor. We received cash to spend, sometimes as much as three hundred dollars. With the ability to determine and experience guilt came the freedom to buy what we wanted, as long as it didn't violate the rules.

At least twice a day all of us were herded into the main house for individual counseling sessions and Circles. Most sessions involved confessions of every little wrongdoing, designed to mold each kid into the institution's concept of a perfect child. Staff would belittle you, and sometimes there were punishments for even the most minor transgressions. This repetition resembled brainwashing and replaced our values, thought processes, and actions with theirs.

On Friday nights there were presentations by invited guest speakers. These were never motivational because they did not conform to the institution's beliefs. To the outside world, Team House promoted the organization as specializing in rehabilitation, so the speakers were from Alcoholics Anonymous, Narcotics Anonymous, and other similar organizations. Our parents would be invited to witness the "wonderful work" they were doing. My mom came often, but she couldn't really separate the good from the bad because she had nothing in her own life experiences to judge by.

Surfing, visits to the beach, plenty of money to spend and beautiful homes to live in—the life we appeared to lead would have been the envy of most kids. But there was a price to pay. The staff's hidden agenda was to wipe our slates clean and insert clones of themselves—much like a cult.

School was way too easy and it was obvious that providing a quality education wasn't a top priority. Nobody complained, though. They brought in an outside teacher. Although I was twelve, I have no idea why she gave me a packet of third grade-level work. I could do all of it in a two-hour sitting and that was all I had to do for the week. Educated people are harder to control, so maybe that was the reason, but I guess I'll never know.

Rather than a good education, Circle was central to all Team House activities. It was how your progress was rated. They were especially interested in your psyche. Were they accomplishing anything in breaking you down, or weren't they? Staff rewarded you for confessions and ratting on your friends' misdoings—the more the better. I learned to get around snitching on others by inventing tales of my own broken rules or bad thoughts. I received credit for them, and how the staff loved it! They had no idea I was playing them along, telling them what they wanted to hear. It was a snap for me—a result of having the best teacher in the world—my father.

Anyway, if they felt you were doing well, you could move up the ladder and get jobs on the outside where you could earn your own money and be allowed more freedom. But all the while, they worked on you by altering your memories and replacing them with new ones, a method used in cults.

Only once did I reach out to the Circle and ask for help with a real problem. It was at a time when I was feeling very vulnerable and suicidal as a result of my still undiagnosed PTSD. Somehow I found the courage to tell the people in the Circle what was going on inside me—the fact that I was thinking of killing myself.

Instead of the support or help I'd hoped to get, all I heard from one of the staff members was, "Okay, so pass the razor blades!" That's like telling someone standing on the ledge of a building to jump. Well, even if they thought that was funny, I was pissed off to no end that my plea for help was met with something as stupid as that. I shouted, "How could you ever say something like that to someone who says they are ready to take their own life? You jerk!" I got up and stomped out of the meeting.

It made them nervous. Although I didn't know it, they had chosen me as their poster child and needed me pliant and fulfilled—the perfect example of a successful rehabilitation. They apologized and made it better, and I played the game. After that the staff let me do whatever I wanted. I was rewarded by being assigned to Zuma House, a beautiful place with massive glass windows that overlooked Zuma Beach. I shared a bedroom with another girl and our room had sliding glass doors that led out to the swimming pool. Somehow I've always known instinctively what I had to do to survive or make my life better. In this case, I did what I had to do to make my life at Team House the best it could be.

After months of surfing, doing arts and surfing some more, I knew my time at Team House had to come to an end. I'd already climbed to almost the top of their ladder and my mom had just gotten out of rehab and moved into a one-bedroom apartment in Pasadena. The programming and brainwashing I saw at this level of Team House was so dark and sadistic, I knew I couldn't allow that to happen to me. I was only thirteen and all the others in my upper level Circle were seventeen and eighteen. Even though I was very young, I knew I had to get out.

I crept out of Zuma House in the middle of the night when everyone was sleeping. I walked the couple of miles to the highway and found a gas station where I used a pay phone to call my mom to pick me up. She came for me right away and welcomed me with open arms. The next day we called my social worker and got permission for me to stay with mom.

Whenever I reflect on my time at Team House I always think of two relationships that have stayed with me my entire life. I met and became friends with a boy named Jameson. He was a couple of years older than me and I finally knew what it felt like to have a big brother that I could trust. Okay, he may not have been my real brother, but to this day we are siblings at heart. He means more to me than blood alone could ever make us. Jameson looked out for me and made me realize everything I'd missed out on with my real brother.

Another relationship began there and would become an important part of my life. Many celebrities volunteered their time at Team House, thinking they were doing good deeds for disadvantaged and troubled kids. Little did they know that this was a mind-control group. One of them was super-star actress Ali MacGraw. I was naive and didn't realize who she was when we first met. For me it was love at first sight, just because she was so nice. She became like a Godmother to me, and because her contribution of money and time was so important to the program, there were no rules or strings attached when I was with her. She took me everywhere. After I escaped from the clutches of Team House, we stayed in touch and became even closer.

The first year I was back with my mother, Ali sent me to Nina Blanchard, an agent for models who appear in major magazines. Miss Blanchard wanted to do a shoot with me but said that I'd have to lose five pounds first. I was already too skinny, got upset, acted childishly, and went home and cried my eyes out.

At fourteen, my internal anger had begun to come out in the form of punching walls and more; and the courts declared me out of control. Ali and my mom felt that it would be therapeutic for me to travel around and visit some of the places I grew up in. Because I'd been on my own since I was eleven and was completely streetwise, and would be staying with former neighbors and people I'd grown up with, they agreed to let me travel alone. They never doubted I could pull it off. With that decision made, Ali bought the bus and plane tickets for my trip.

In San Diego, I found the house I had lived in to age nine or ten was empty. I discovered that someone had left a window unlocked and I let myself inside. I climbed the stairs to what had been my little girl pink bedroom. To my surprise, the room was still pink. I lay down on the floor and hoped that if another little girl lived here someday, her lot in life would be better than mine. In my mind's eye I saw my parents fighting at the end of the hallway, and it was as though I could hear the sounds of my dad's truck or Harley as he pulled into the driveway. The hours slipped by, but somehow I couldn't move. I stayed in that room half of the night, lying on the floor, trying to ignore the tears that dampened my cheeks.

I was old enough to want to try to figure out how I became the person I was. I felt a need to locate people who had known me when I was little. I was able to find one of the social workers who worked with my whole family when I was small. I stayed with that woman for a week, went places with her family, ate dinner with them and learned a lot about those early years. She was wonderfully frank about answering every question I asked her.

I wanted to know how she saw me as a child. Imagine my shock when she said, "I saw you as a little girl who could poison her parents' coffee and walk away like nothing happened."

It wasn't what I expected to hear. Surely I wouldn't have killed them. It hit me like a punch to the stomach, but when I got over the gut-wrenching feeling and thought rationally, I realized what she really saw was total withdrawal and disassociation. At the time she knew me, I'd already gone beyond feeling emotion and my protective shield was firmly in place.

That trip to my old neighborhoods brought much closure for me. And I believe it also prepared me for the next major chapter in my life: Hollywood. Once the allure of Tinseltown got under my skin, it fueled my nature as a rebel and I did things I never thought I would be capable of.

CHAPTER EIGHT

I was so happy to be away from Team House, my spirits were soaring. Living with my mom was working out okay. We were getting along and I went to the AA meetings with her as she tried to regain control of her life.

My first big emotional test came when I saw my brother again. He had joined the Navy and was stationed nearby in Long Beach. Although I hadn't seen him in at least three years, he had kept in touch with our mother. If I said I was confused about seeing him again, that would have been the understatement of the year. The first time he came to the apartment I wanted to try to have a relationship with this young man called my brother, and I guess that's what made me put aside all of the resentment I felt and give him a hug.

When he walked in the door I was struck by how much bigger he was. He had always been good looking, and now he was buff and gorgeous. At six feet six, he was like a handsome Incredible Hulk. He'd become so muscular I was pretty sure he was on some sort of steroids, and his temper was short and he was very snappy. I tried to tell myself that was just the way he was, but finally asked if he was using steroids. He not only admitted it—he bragged about it and strutted around showing off his body.

He and his Navy friends began to drop by the apartment quite often. After a few months they suggested we go to a bar. Even though I was only fourteen, I did look old enough to get served. They introduced me to a place called Nardis. The first thing that struck me was that there were no women in this bar. I thought, "How friendly, these guys are all hanging out together." Of course, that was as naive as it could get. I needed to be hit over the head to realize I was in a gay bar. I wasn't asked for ID and by being my normal chatty self, Jacob, the owner, befriended me as the only real female in the bar. It remained one of my favorite hangouts until it was torn down years later.

My brother had another shock in store for me. He had a specific reason for going to that bar—to gay bash. It was a Halloween night and one of the gay men was dressed as a black person. My brother struck up a conversation with him, and then without any provocation punched him in the face. I was so shocked by what he'd just done I could barely move or say anything, but my brother grabbed me and pulled me out the door. He and his friends were bragging and laughing about bashing the gay guy as we drove back to the apartment. It was then I realized why they took me there—to watch them raise Hell, and I resented what he'd done. I'm sure he never went back to Nardis, but I did.

To my surprise, the next day he apologized and expressed guilt over what he'd done to me from the time I was a little kid. I never thought I'd hear that from anybody, much less him. I tried to like him after that, but eventually we just went our separate ways. I felt guilty for a while about not being able to fully forgive him. But it is what it is.

I'd met two gay friends named Jeff and Bud through a mutual friend. They were a lot older than me and I loved being around them because it was safe, not like my abusive experiences with men. One night they suggested we all hang out together and the first place that came to mind was Nardis.

I'd been declared an out-of-control teen, and with my Mom's history she just let me do what I wanted. So Nardis became a regular place for me to spend time, usually with Jeff and Bud. Thankfully, Jacob didn't hold what my brother had done against me, and we actually became good friends. He never found out how old I really was. When I think back now, I could have cost him his business license.

When I was fifteen I got a job babysitting for a couple who were friends of my mom's and lived less than a mile from us. Their next door neighbor, a hairstylist to celebrities, was a 30-year-old straight man named Gus, who was raising his young daughter alone. Sure, I was basically still a kid myself, but with everything I'd gone through in those fifteen rough years, my soul was much older. It hit me full-on, that combination of attraction and the awesome feeling that this older man was interested in me. It didn't take long for him to become my first real love and eventually the father of my first daughter.

Shortly after meeting Gus, I turned sixteen and Ali thought with my love of dancing it would be a wonderful idea to send me to the famous American Academy of Dramatic Arts in Pasadena. She paid my tuition, but I had to pass an audition to get admitted. I aced it and I loved the dancing and worked my butt off at it. The problem for me was the acting, which was required curriculum. My attention span just didn't cut it. I had to drop out and never went back.

When Ali was active in my life, we talked on the phone for hours at a time, telling each other stories. And then her house in Malibu burned down. After losing everything important to her, she moved to New Mexico where she began a whole new spiritual life for herself. I love that woman to this day and I always will.

***

When a young girl's mind is filled with romance, her decisions are not the same as an adult's. I was in love with Gus. Forget that in many respects I was still a child and he was a man. I loved the idea of being in love, and it didn't take much for me to move in with him. My mother's "hands-off" attitude meant she didn't interfere, and soon Gus and I were living as a couple.

We had a very wonderful relationship. He was an outdoors kind of guy with a spiritual nature. His clients loved him and included him on their social calendars. Rather than Nardis, I was now attending the many star-studded functions we were invited to. If they had known how young I was, it could have been a problem for him, so I always had to keep my age a secret to avoid causing any embarrassment. With my hair done in the latest style and hot clothes, there was no way they had any idea I was younger than the eighteen we told them. Gus made sure I looked like appropriate eye-candy for a guy like him.

Because of his love for the outdoors we went camping a lot. One of my fondest memories is when he took me camping in Northern California for my 18th birthday. Our site was on a mountain ledge overlooking the beach with lush forest and creeks behind us. It was breathtaking. We enjoyed life and didn't lack for anything. Barbecued lobster tails and steaks were the rule, not the exception.

I was so happy that I decided to let my dad know about my new life. Even though there was no way I could ever live with him again after all that had happened, on the other side of his violent nature I was still his little girl and he was my best friend, so other than the nine months I was in Connie's foster home, we kept in touch by phone. When I called him with my announcement about Gus, it was greeted by total silence. And with my father, unlike most people, it was what he didn't say that said it all. The lack of a response and his refusal to meet Gus sent a very scary message that I understood all too well. He didn't wish the man who was living with his little girl well. In fact, he'd just as soon see him dead.

After that conversation, I knew I had to impress upon Gus how serious this could be. I explained to him that my father was used to getting whatever he wanted by any means necessary and getting away with it. I made my point. Gus accepted the fact that my father was a dangerous man and one or both of our lives could be in danger. Gus had a gun collection we used for target shooting. He gave me a small handgun and told me to keep it hidden in the pickup truck that he let me drive. He selected another gun from his collection to carry himself, and from that time we were always armed. He even slept with a gun under his pillow. How awful is that, to have to arm yourself against an attack by your own father?

One day when Gus was leaving for work, a man came out of the bushes near our house. As Gus told me later, the man's face was covered with some sort of cloth and he was wearing gloves. Before Gus could drive away, a shot zinged into the windshield in front of him, cracking it, but not going through. The theory was that the bullet must have struck the glass at an angle that caused it to deflect rather than penetrate. Otherwise, it would have been a perfect head shot. We both figured the shooter was one of my dad's puppets who would do anything the Puppet Master asked him to.

We decided not to make a report to the police because I was sure my dad was behind the incident. And, as I'd learned the hard way, when my dad was involved, the cops did nothing anyway.

I'd grown up a lot over the years and wasn't as afraid of my dad threatening my own safety as I might have been a few years before. I knew in my heart that Gus was his target, and not me. So when he came to town with the step-bitch a few weeks after the shooting and asked me to take a ride with them in her convertible, I went. This wasn't a time to run away from reality—I had to face it. The step-bitch was in the front with him. I mentioned the shooting and she reacted with shock. It may have been faked, but I really don't think she knew my dad was responsible. But Dad didn't bat an eyelash; he stared straight ahead as though I'd said nothing. No concern, no surprise, and no reassurance that he would protect me. I didn't need it because Gus was the one he wanted to kill.

One night Gus and I were drinking and got into a heated argument. My mom was working the midnight shift at a nearby grocery store, so I went to see her at about one in the morning. But she was busy with her job and couldn't do anything to help me.

I decided to call Gus from a payphone outside the store before I went home, because I didn't want to walk back into a bad situation. If there was anything I'd learned over the years, it was to test the waters before jumping in. Just about the time we'd begun to speak, a couple of guys got out of their car that was parked near the phone. I noticed that another guy remained in the backseat of the vehicle and a girl was in the front passenger seat. The two guys, who appeared to be in their twenties, high on who knows what, grabbed the handset from me and began ranting at Gus. "We've got your girlfriend. We heard her talking to you and you're not shit," they hollered. The more they talked, the more scared I became, but the madder Gus got. Finally he told them to come meet him at a 7-Eleven by our house in South Pasadena. "You can talk to my gun," he told them.

They threatened me and told me to get into my truck and lead them to the 7-Eleven. My heart was pounding so hard I could feel it slamming against my ribs. I did what they said. I drove.

Before I got into the truck I glanced at their car and

found the girl glaring at me through her open window. Her expression was smug and she appeared to be enjoying the terror her friends were putting me through. As I drove, I kept seeing the girl's face in my mind and my fear turned to anger. For the first time in my life I wanted to hurt another person. I lowered my window and motioned for them to pull along side of me. When they did I told them to pull the fuck over.

After we were stopped I hid my gun underneath the seat cover to make sure things didn't get totally out of control, and then I jumped out of the truck. I raced to their car and yanked the girl's door open. I grabbed the bitch by her hair and started hitting her. Two of the guys tried to pull me away from her, but I threw them both off and then started beating her in the face. Her expression wasn't smug any longer! With adrenaline pumping like a bellows igniting a fire, rage took over and all I could think of was that these people were a threat to what I'd come to think of as my normal life. *They were going to pay.*

The guys got up and came back at me. In the melee they tore my shirt off. I didn't even flinch. I just kept on punching the girl. She started crying and pleading for her life and that brought me back to my senses. My rage subsided and I stopped swinging. As I calmed down I stood over her and stared down at her bloody face, shocked at what I'd done. What kind of a person was I turning into? When I drove away they didn't follow and I never saw any of them again.

Knowing Gus would be at the 7-Eleven, I drove there with my shirt in tatters and abrasions on my knuckles. I was still pissed off about what had happened and took it out on Gus. I slapped him around a little bit while shouting that this wouldn't have happened if we hadn't fought. We both realized what a bizarre situation that was and laughed those nervous laughs like people do when they know they're safe. Our argument was forgotten.

The next morning I was talking to my mom on the

phone and told her about the fight. I said I wasn't hurt, just a small scratch on my chest from when they ripped off my shirt. But as we talked I realized my period was late. Could it be? I went to my mom's and took a pregnancy test. It was positive. I went to a clinic and had another test done. The result was the same—I was pregnant. We had wanted to have a baby for three years and it was finally going to happen! The idea of sealing our love with a baby made Gus and me very happy.

On March 31, 1992 Marie was born. She was healthy and beautiful. I was ecstatic. But my euphoria didn't last very long because shortly afterward Gus graduated from smoking a little pot once in a while and started using crack. I was real naive then when it came to crack, but I knew he had changed. He turned mean. He started spending most of his nights in the bathroom by himself and he wasn't attentive to Marie or me.

There had been too much abuse in my life and I just couldn't let it happen again. I knew there was only one solution—I had to break off our relationship and get away, at least for a while. I packed some things for myself and the baby and we took a plane to Arizona where we spent a couple of weeks with my aunt. After some time had passed, I returned to California and moved back in with my mother. As for Gus, people we knew told me he was very sad, but he didn't fight to get us back. Instead, as time went on he fell into a life centered on his next high. I often wonder if our love would have survived if it hadn't been for the crack.

After Gus, Nardis again became my regular place to hang out while my mom watched Marie for me. Aretha Franklin was my favorite singer and they had a lot of her songs on the juke box. I'd go there and spend time laughing and joking with Jeff and Bud and whoever else was there. I called it my "Cheers" because it was the place where everybody knows your name.

During that time I was so passionate about Aretha's music, I'd be there standing on the bar screaming, "Who's the Queen of Soul?" I could do anything there and get away with it. And all the regulars watched out for me and made sure I wasn't bothered. I also danced a lot and played pool there. Having grown up with a pool table in my house I knew how to handle a cue stick. My preference, though, was to play darts. I loved the place and the people because that was where I could be the "other me," the one without a care in the world who just loved to dance and have fun. For those few hours, I didn't have to carry the weight of experiences kids and teens should never be victim to. My gay friends loved me with no strings attached. My daughter Marie was the one thing I'd gotten right in life, and when the evening was over, I went back to being a teenage mom.

Years later when I was working on the Strip, I'd have my driver take me to Nardis in my limo, bodyguards and all. And because it was a beer bar I always brought my own champagne.

While I was still 18, one of my older friends gave me her driver's license to use for ID and I started going to the West Hollywood clubs with Jeff and Bud. If my friend's license didn't fool the bouncer and I couldn't get inside, the guys would go into the bathroom, open a window and let me get in that way. I loved the dancing in those clubs. I'd dance, and dance, and dance some more. Through my dancing I became popular. It wasn't hard for me at all.

As much as I enjoyed the club life, I knew that I had to do something to get my life back on track. As a first step I took the test for admission to Pasadena Community College and scored above average. I took a class in Women's History, but my memory issues made it extremely difficult for me. Still, I pushed and pushed, but it was just too much for me and I had to give it up. My time at PCC wasn't wasted, though. While there I met Jennifer, my future roommate. She worked for the FBI in an intake unit that separated the sane from the crazies. Jennifer is a strong Christian and we bonded immediately. We have remained very close to this day and she has never stopped praying for me. She has never judged me for any of the situations I got into and has been a faithful friend to me for over twenty years.

Jeff, Bud and I went full force into the club scene. I danced and ran into the clubs as if I owned them. It was a "home" type of feeling. Marie and I moved out of my mother's and in with Jennifer. We were living well. I enrolled in an optical training program and in a year was certified to make lenses and fit glasses.

When I finished school I got a job in an optician's office in Beverly Hills, but became bored fast. Even the part-time job I got at an Italian restaurant didn't do the trick. When it came to work, nothing seemed to satisfy me. And then one night I went to the Coconut Teaser on the Strip. Inside was an after-hours nightclub I'll just call "The Club." When I walked in there it was as if Destiny took over. That very night I got a job doing promotion for The Club. At last I'd found my niche; and that's when I surrendered my soul to the Sunset Strip.

CHAPTER NINE

My first night in The Club just blew me away. I felt a spiritual connection from the moment I walked in. Like what had happened previously in my life, there was a gut feeling this was meant to be. I managed to get an introduction to the DJ, who was also the boss. I'll keep it simple and refer to him as "DJ." He was a handsome man about five-feet-nine, with his dark black hair pulled into a ponytail. Without blinking an eye I asked him for a job promoting The Club.

He looked at me and said, "You must be kidding. What makes you think you can do that?"

I sensed right away that our relationship was both mental and spiritual; and my smile had some mischief behind it when I answered, "Because I'm someone who can weed out the tweakers and bring in the artists. You can't believe how many people I know all over the city and have been told I'm a 'people magnet.'" Most people would have quizzed me before telling me to get lost, but I wasn't even surprised when he asked me a few questions and said I had the job.

That night I started dancing and getting a feel for the place. After all, you have to know what will make people want to come and then come back. Don't get the idea I was on the brink of making lots of money, because I wasn't. It wasn't about the money, though. By the time the evening was over, it was more about feeling like I had found a spiritual base and a home.

At that time, I had no idea what The Club would come to mean to me. And DJ was real easy to work with, even though in the beginning he struck me as being a little arrogant. But it was what I call an innocent arrogance. And even with his trademark smirk, he wasn't stuck up or mean. It was just part of his personality.

When I was around him I could always be "me." Regardless of what I did or said, he was there to support me emotionally—something I'd never had my entire life. In fact I even allowed myself to be snotty to him sometimes. Like one time he walked past me and told me part of my job was to pick up some trash from the floor. I smiled at him with a look that clearly said, "Are you nuts?" Out loud I said, "That's not my job."

Had I said that to my father, I would have landed against a wall at the other side of the room. But, with DJ, guess what? He bent down and picked it up himself. That's how it was between us. Oh, I was just being cocky because by then I had developed a deep connection with him and we worked so well together.

Dance partners I'd acquired as I moved from club to club included some executives from Disney, high-profile art gallery owners, affluent business owners and a whole array of other people whose connections had connections. I don't know why, but somehow I was always dealing with the top dogs. When I was little I reached for the top of the heap and my mother cautioned me not to set my expectations so high. My answer was always, "But that's where I belong, Mom." On top of that, some of my friends promoted popular after-hours clubs, so in other words, I was plugged into the right people and was able to bring a lot of artists into The Club. Just as I had at Nardis, DJ and I had created what you might describe as an after-hours version of Cheers, complete with dancing, drugs and philosophy.

You see, in those early morning hours when the intensity that was Hollywood finally came to rest like a tired child, The Club came to life. If you watched closely, groups of people gravitated into the same triangular formation in the center of the dance floor every evening. At the same time, an aura of immorality, malicious power struggles and greed emanated from the very center of the dancing throng, like something slimy waiting to strike. No one seemed to react visibly and at first I didn't recognize it either.

Later whenever that happened, I'd signal DJ and he'd insert a subliminal sound of angels, or church bells or doves to signal good rather than evil. It may sound strange, but gradually the dancers moved from the triangle into a circle and the bad vibes disappeared.

I'm sure that up and coming stars went in and out of The Club all the time, but with my memory challenges from the traumatic brain injury of my childhood, I couldn't even tell you who they were. There was a glimmer of recognition, but it was like the flicker of a flame. There for a minute, then gone. Surprisingly, even when I went back to the Strip after being gone for ten years and The Club no longer existed, I told the operators of some of the current venues who I was and my name still carried weight. I was put on the VIP list immediately and thanked for paving the way for them.

In my early days of working at The Club new promoters realized that just like them I wasn't making much money from bringing in the crowds. Some who didn't even know me ridiculed me.

I'd hear comments like, "What's the matter with you? Don't you know the other guys are making the money while you work your ass off?" Or, maybe, "Yeah, someone else would ask to be paid what they're worth. But not you, Baby."

As time went on they realized I'd become a force to be reckoned with. Each morning after DJ finished spinning records at nine a.m., I quit working the crowd, stood next to him and danced only for him. Like I said before, it definitely wasn't about the money. In my heart I knew I'd finally found what I loved doing, and at long last life seemed good.

Having said that, it's important for you to understand why The Club was different than all the others along the Strip. Many of the customers told me they hadn't experienced true joy until coming there. And for some it was a life-changer. My friend Avi is a good example of that and even though I've been gone from that life for several years now, Avi and I have stayed connected.

Avi is one of the old crowd who considers his life was changed through knowing us. He said but for a twist of fate he never would have found us. He'd never even heard of The Club until one morning around 4 a.m. when he was leaving another after-hours joint. He noticed his shoe was untied. He bent down to tie it and spotted one of our flyers on the sidewalk. He thought, "Why not?" Not long afterward he was at The Club.

In some of the deep conversations we had later, Avi told me he grew up with the thought that emotions were of no use. That if you showed emotion it was a way for people to hurt you and take advantage of you. He explained to me, "Because of the way I was brought up, thinking only about possessions and with the accumulation of things so strongly ingrained in my being, I grew to hate putting myself on the market just for money to buy things. In fact I hated my life so much that I cried. But the first time I went to The Club I didn't get the negative sensations I got in the other places—everything was positive. Hanging out there caused my whole attitude to change. The Club is what kept me alive. I know that sounds dramatic, but until I found it I didn't know how to think or feel any other way."

Avi went on to get his degree in drug and alcohol counseling.

Like Avi, there were many others who came to The Club and found the courage to help others and find fulfillment.

Sometimes I brought a few of my dance partners from other night spots back to The Club and we'd tear up the dance floor. Sadly, I lost many of them to the underworld of drugs and porno. It always broke my heart, as though somewhere up above you could hear the angels crying. However, it is what it is and you just have to keep on going, even when tragedy strikes. So, I kept on moving, hoping this newfound joy in life would last forever.

As time went by and I became better known and more popular, guys tried to hit on me. Sometimes they became annoying and even threatening. I remember one night a guy in line told me that if I spent an hour with him, no sex involved, he'd give me two grand. I told him he had just treated me like a whore. If he'd have asked me to a movie, I might have said "yes." Because of incidents like that I came to realize that my job often placed me in a vulnerable position and I needed a bodyguard with me at all times. I was done being the victim and began taking every precaution to protect myself from danger or abuse.

But overall, I loved most of the customers. And even though I was still very young myself, I treated them as if they were my own children. Sometimes I'd be on the balcony at The Club with a crowd fully engaged in philosophical conversations about unraveling the mysteries of angels and God. This was a vital period of time for me spiritually; and it was all happening while I was in the midst of the inherent evil that existed in the belly of my new after-hours world.

Every evening before I came to work I texted DJ with our 111 code, which meant I was almost there. I'd actually reached celebrity status with the Sunset Strip throng in such a short time that on some nights DJ greeted me at the front door for my grand entrance. I felt like royalty when they moved the line out of the way and DJ escorted me through the crowd. He was one of the few people who could handle my outrageous personality.

Like those messages that flash on movie screens to make you buy a product, together DJ and I chose the lighting and subliminals that made our club the best. We used elements like the bells and spiritual sounds in the backbeats, to combat the immorality and replace it with good. Just to clarify, the backbeats are what hit your subconscious while the main music plays.

When I was at The Club I danced; I was an artist and a messenger. I knew I was exactly where God wanted me to be at that moment in time. I guess for me it was like being in Heaven while my body and soul were still on earth.

CHAPTER TEN

The year was 1996 and by now I'd taken on two additional clubs, Club Diva and Club Desire, besides working at the 8240 Sunset club, Roxbury North across the street, and The Club inside the Coconut Teaser on the corner. As an artist who loves to bring visions to life, my canvas is covered with my thoughts, plans, and dreams, until they finally become reality. The clubs I created were my paintings.

I'd only been on the job about four weeks when a fellow named Steve came into The Club and said he wanted me to meet his partner Peter, the main club owner along the Strip. He was headquartered at 8240 Sunset across from the Roxbury. He not only owned that building, but was the major investor in the Roxbury and other clubs. He was reputed to be the most powerful moneyed promoter on the strip.

Peter's proposition was straight-forward. He wanted me to work the clubs at both 8240 and the Roxbury. The new jobs carried a lot more responsibility because I would be hiring the promoters, bartenders, security, DJs and whatever it took to make the clubs run. As part of my agreement with Peter he wanted me to give up the other clubs. I let Club Diva and Club Desire go. The only one I refused to give up was

The Club.

It was payoff time and at last I was being rewarded for what I did. But because of my problems handling money and numbers caused by the beatings I had suffered as a kid, the majority of my compensation wasn't in cash, which was fine with me. I was free to use my creativity and not have to grapple with day-to-day personal finances.

Peter provided me with my own office at 8240 and paid for my apartment in the building next door. Although I still had my place in Pasadena, the apartment gave me a place to rest and refresh without having to make the commute. The clubs were producing lots of revenue which he used to cover the costs for my bodyguards, limo, and virtually my every need. And when I did require cash, it was there. That allowed me to continue at The Club as a work of love, not money. Everything there was about the art, and that's where I excelled. The success of The clubs was proof of that.

Although most of them were within walking distance of my apartment, for security purposes my method of transportation to and from work was a limo and bodyguards. And when I wasn't working and wanted to go to Pasadena or elsewhere I had my friend Lacy, whom I'd met at Nardis years earlier, pick me up and I would ride with her. She was always there for me.

It's important I point out in addition to the aura of glamour and mystique hovering over the after-hours club scene on the Strip, it is an industry with guns everywhere, drugs, graft and more. If you were part of it, you had to be a gangster, and that's what I became. During the mid-1990s I was the only woman who had managed to reach star status in the exciting, hyped world of after-hours clubs along Hollywood's famed Sunset Strip. And to this day no other female has accomplished what I did with that crowd. I'm still proud of that. I cherish the fact that I didn't fuck my way to the top, either. I did it the old-fashioned way—I worked for it! Hollywood was only a piece of a chapter in Peter's life, but it was a part of my being. These were my people who came from my cities.

As hectic as it was, my work at 8240 and Roxbury never slowed me down at The Club. Let's just say I sort of became a mama figure to the lost souls who drifted in and out of the place.

Things were going great for me and got even better when one night Peter showed up in the limo and asked me to take a ride with him. He said he had a surprise for me and that I'd have to wear a blindfold during the drive. It was weird, but also exciting. We drove for forty minutes or so and after the limo stopped Peter guided me into a building. When he removed my blindfold I was stunned. I was in the middle of a huge, beautiful room with a high ceiling and a stage the size of a house. I learned later that we were in a club named Roxbury South in Orange County near Disneyland, in which Peter was a minority owner. Confused, I looked at him questioningly. He smiled and said, "It's all yours. You can do whatever you want with it."

I was having issues with Peter because of his tremendous ego and was becoming very disenchanted with him. I knew that somewhere along the line he'd end up taking credit for whatever I did for The Club. In spite of that I appreciated this new opportunity he was giving me and was excited about it.

Peter introduced me to Jason, the main owner. I liked him and felt he was someone I would be able to work well with. It was agreed that I'd develop a plan for how I felt The Club should be run and present it to Jason. If he liked my ideas, I'd start managing Roxbury South. I was ecstatic, but my euphoria was short-lived.

A few days later I was standing in my office at 8240 Sunset prior to going to Roxbury South to present my proposals to Jason. I was dressed to impress in a floor length spandex-like dress. It had a slit up the side and you could see my black stockings. My shoes were shiny red with black bottoms. My hair was done perfectly into a French roll with curls hanging down. But looks aside, I was feeling pretty beat up and was ready to just mellow out a little.

The phone rang and my stepmother, the last person in the world I expected to hear from, was on the line. What was she doing calling me at The Club of all places?

"Do you have someone with you?" she asked.

I lied and said, "yes."

"Are you sitting down?"

Before I could answer, she said, "Your father passed away a couple of days ago. I'm sorry I didn't let you know sooner."

In that moment, everything crashed around me. My father might have been the reason I was so rebellious, but he was my world. After all the years I had fought to prove myself to him, it was as though my purpose in life died with her words.

My head was spinning. Barely a week had passed since I'd gotten into some real trouble and made a phone call to him.

I hadn't told him the situation I was in then, because in my eyes I'd gotten myself into it and had to get myself out of it. It wasn't like he would have come to my rescue, anyway. Damn it! In that last call he finally said the words I'd yearned to hear for so many years. "I am proud of you and I'll be there in two weeks to see your clubs." And now that would never happen.

Memories of recent phone calls with my father flashed through my mind. Every Sunday after closing the clubs, I used to sit on the floor and talk with him for hours. During some of those calls I read psalms from the Bible as my tears fell. I knew his tears fell, too, because I could hear him crying, but when my stepmother was around, his demeanor changed and he would say he had to hang up. The woman was so evil. I knew that by opening up to me, he was feeling hurt in his heart and in the process, finally becoming human. And now that was gone, too.

Regaining my composure I asked, "How did he die?"

"His stomach ruptured in the middle of the night. They called it a bleed and rupture."

That explanation was believable to me because of his drinking and prior stomach surgeries. The red flags wouldn't come until I got to his house the next day and realized some things weren't right. That's when I learned my stepmother had him cremated right after his death. *Why the rush?*

And she had bodyguards all around her to protect her from—me. *Why would I want to hurt her?*

Add to that the fact that she sold their million-dollar house right in front of my face before the memorial service. Okay, I can write off one of these things as coincidence, but not all three.

But when she uttered those words to me over the phone I didn't know about the cremation, the bodyguards, or selling the house. I didn't have anything to say to her and I remember falling to my knees, picking up my chair and throwing it into the wall. I let out a scream that the whole Strip probably heard. "He's dead, my Daddy's dead." You know, I can still feel the hurt, the tremendous pain I experienced that day.

My father's death really threw me for a loop. I loved him so much and even though I knew he was bad, I was able to see the good in him. Initially, I was so disassociated from the reality of the loss that I yelled, but didn't cry. It wasn't until later in life that the tears poured for a whole day.

People were always offering me drugs in exchange for letting them enter the clubs. I did speed for a couple years to keep up with my three-day work sprees and I drank some. I wasn't into taking all the drugs everyone else was—although

I did take Ecstasy a few times to lower my blood pressure. So I had a pretty impressive stash built up that included Quaaludes, crack, coke, heroin—you name it, I had it. After visiting the step-bitch I was very angry at losing the man whose respect I craved the most. I told myself I had the balls to die, too. I started using the drugs and didn't stop until they were all gone two days later. My meltdown was complete.

At this point my mom and I had gone our separate ways and didn't communicate much. It wasn't until after I'd taken every last drug and pill that I called her. Having now experienced her type of drug Hell for myself, I had a small amount of empathy for her when I said, "It's detox or death."

She called my boyfriend, who at the time was West Arkeen, the writer for Guns and Roses. West is deceased now, but when my mother reached out to him he got some money together and they found this little Ritz hotel-type rehab in Monrovia that admitted me in the middle of the night.

I've been told I was very combative when I got there, but I don't remember much about that night. However, I do recall pushing a guy up against the wall saying, "Men think with their dicks."

They assigned me to a room with another resident named Tessa, who was also in for detox. She is now a Public Defender and remains one of my very best friends to this day; and I am Godmother to her daughter Marly. But when we first met, Tessa's attitude toward me was, if she wants to go back to Hollywood, let her.

I had so many drugs in me that I didn't know what was up and what was down. I kept yelling one thing which was the truth, "They should have had real medical care here."

I finally fell asleep and woke up two days later, still in my clothes. I had peed in the bed and that's how I know nobody even checked on me. Tessa told me that I went to bed a bitch and woke up an angel. What a hoot. I was wearing my smile and said good morning to everyone. I was back to myself. Tessa had lost her own father and could relate to how I was feeling. That really helped us to bond.

While I was undergoing treatment, my displeasure with Peter festered. I kept thinking about that big ego of his and how he took all the credit while I did all the work. He'd bring in other business people and use me as eye candy while he showed off my work as his own. But Peter didn't have the artist inside of him that I did and everybody knew it. And I could write business plans in a matter of hours that would have taken him all year to complete.

In a couple of weeks I was somewhat back on my feet and called Peter from the payphone in the detox facility. My anger toward him was boiling over. I wanted to scare him and said I was going to call the Feds and spill my guts about the after-hours clubs. I was lying like crazy and really don't know what I'd have told them even if I did call. But I said, "This is the end for me and the end for you." I was only bluffing and fully intended to return to the clubs when I was able. But apparently I was too convincing because Peter didn't just get worried—he ran. He did a vanishing act!

I found that out several weeks later when I was released from detox. Tessa and I took a drive along the Strip and saw the other club owners standing outside on the street. We stopped and I asked them what happened. They told me they didn't know the reason, just that Peter took everything—all the money and equipment— and disappeared. With everything gone there was no way they could stay in business.

I was laughing on the inside about Peter, but I was sad, too, because in my desire to hurt him I had destroyed my own life as well. I had the empty feeling that comes when you've made your mark and then everything has been taken away from you. I'd put my heart into those clubs. Not just a little of my heart, all of my heart. So with them not existing anymore, in a weird way it was like a very emotional romantic break up.

The Club at 8240 was shut down. The Coconut Teaser stayed open for several years, but was eventually closed as a business decision. The Roxbury had so many silent owners that they struggled for awhile, but eventually got on their feet. You'd be amazed how many people dream of owning and running a club of their own, but never discover the secret to attracting the customers who make it profitable.

So Peter was out and so was I. But before I left the club scene I wrote No More Crying Angels©, a song I'm very proud of. I knew a lot of people in the music business, and many of them wanted to buy the lyrics, but I didn't feel the time was right to put them to music.

I wrote as I watched the sun come up on the Sunset Strip. That was such a free feeling—like you had the world in your hands.

PART TWO
From Hollywood to the Hood

CHAPTER ELEVEN

With the clubs gone, my life had changed radically and my thoughts turned in other directions. I guess somewhere deep down, even though my father was dead, I still felt a compulsion to fulfill his expectations. That meant making more Italian babies and keeping the family bloodline going.

West and I were no longer together and since leaving rehab I had been living with my friend Tessa in a townhouse in Burbank. With our fresh, sober attitudes we decided to take a road trip to Oregon with our kids—my daughter Marie and Tessa's son Michael. The result was so hilarious we wrote a journal and presented it to her uptight Jewish family.

They welcomed me like one of their own children, and the feeling of belonging filled in some of the pieces missing in my life. After so many years of not knowing what it was like to have fun or experience normal relationships, I loved this new existence and found it wonderful bringing people and things to life. I guess you could say I finally had a shine. Maybe God had answered my prayers at last.

Still, I had this need to find an Italian man I could fall in love with and have those babies to honor my father. At the end of 1996, I met Angelo on one of the first chat lines to debut on the internet. He was Italian, lived in Boston and was a computer genius who worked as an IT manager at a medical facility. He lived up to all the criteria I'd listed for a potential relationship, and within two months he quit his job and came to California to meet me.

When I saw him, my first thought was he could have been a poster child for the Goodfellas-type of handsome, slightly over six feet tall with a little bald spot just beginning to show in his thick brown hair. His eyes were hazel and he had generous lips—a really good-looking guy.

We fell in love right away and he returned to Boston to pack up the rest of his stuff. In November 1996, we were married with a full Roman Catholic wedding mass in a little town in Northern California called LeMoore. We stayed there with Marie's former nanny for a few months after the wedding, and then moved into an apartment in San Pedro, in Southern California.

Tessa was heartbroken when I got married. We'd had such a happy period of time laughing, cooking and traveling together, and now she thought I was abandoning her and our friendship. I assured her that was not the case and pointed out that San Pedro was not very far away. Looking back now, those were really the happiest days of my life. Angelo seemed so normal then. He loved my daughter Marie. She loved him and she automatically began to call him Dad. Later he made it official by formally adopting her.

My one concern was that Angelo told me he was affiliated with organized crime. He didn't provide a lot of detail at that time, but I knew if we were to have a successful marriage, he needed to cut those ties. He agreed and as far as I knew that was the end of it.

I got pregnant with Rosemary, my second daughter, pretty quickly. I don't know why, but it seems that everything in my life has been a life or death situation and her birth was no exception.

You know how sometimes you just sense something isn't quite right but don't have a clue as to why? On the night before Thanksgiving, 1997, I was in the middle of making dinner and suddenly overcome with a feeling that something was wrong. In my heart, I knew I had to get to the hospital. Dinner would just have to wait.

I shut everything off and drove myself to the emergency room. The doctor checked me and said everything seemed okay, but something made him decide to admit me and monitor the baby's head by passing a monitor through my cervix. The baby was getting zero percent oxygen and I was rushed into surgery. Angelo made it to the hospital just before they operated. When the baby was delivered, she wasn't breathing and it took over six minutes to revive her. The mere fact that she survived made her a miracle baby.

The need I felt to get to the hospital is one of those things you can't explain. I'd had no symptoms—just an inner voice demanding I take action. If I hadn't listened to that angel talking to me, Rosemary would not be here today. The only times I ever saw Angelo cry were when his kids were born and when I left him. That night Angelo cried, but then things changed.

We had been married just over a year, yet after Rosemary was born our sex life became practically non-existent. And with increasing frequency Angelo didn't come home until several hours after he left work; and sometimes he didn't make it home at all. On each occasion he refused to explain where he had been. About the same time, parking tickets began to arrive in the mail showing the violations occurred at an address I didn't recognize. I tried to ignore what was happening and pretend everything was okay.

But after awhile I couldn't ignore the signs any longer: my husband was seeing another woman. I had been hurt too often when I was little to disregard the obvious. I had to know for sure. One thing was certain, though. No money could buy me. Nothing could make me stay if my suspicions were true, because I would just end up hating Angelo and resenting him, and that didn't feel right to me.

For several years I'd known a supervising detective in South Bureau Homicide who worked with a whole bunch of gang programs in LA. I called him and told him what was going on. He took me under his wing and introduced me to an attorney who was opening his own firm in San Pedro. In fact, they were still unpacking boxes.

I told him why I suspected Angelo was having an affair, contrary to the illusion of our supposedly happy marriage. This particular attorney was a hardliner when it came to wandering husbands and recommended that I consider divorcing Angelo. As we talked, the conversation turned to his opening the new office. He said I'd need an income and to my surprise offered me a clerical job there. With my background in running clubs, I would never have thought of myself doing that kind of work, but knew he was right and I accepted. My philosophy has always been you do what you have to in order to survive.

The hard part was telling Angelo I knew he was cheating on me. He was the kind of guy who would try to bluff his way through and demand to know what made me accuse him of something like that. So I decided to say my friend Robert, a P.I., had been following him. I gave him the address on the parking tickets, but never told him where I'd gotten it. I let him think Robert had seen him there.

True to form, he shouted, "I'll sue that damn PI. He's slandering me and I haven't done anything wrong."

I stood right up to him and shouted back, "Robert doesn't lie. If he saw you with a woman at that address, then that's what he saw." I scribbled Robert's number on a piece of paper and threw it at him. "Here. This is his number. Call him and accuse him, you cheating bastard."

Seeing how positive I was that he'd been seen, he

backed down and admitted to the affair.

The thought that my husband, the one person who was supposed to be pure in my life, could do something like this made me so angry I grabbed a hammer and began to take whacks at his precious computer, but I didn't unplug it first. When smoke and sparks began to fly, I snatched the computer and ran downstairs to the trash bin in case it was about to catch fire. Then I kicked him out of the house, found a sitter and went to church.

Angelo and I didn't communicate for awhile, but eventually we did talk. He told me he'd found God and was ready to do whatever it took for our marriage to work, including going to counseling. I agreed to give it another try, but it wasn't easy.

Week after week I sat in counseling with him saying, "I hate him." He took it, though, and we stayed with it. After six months, forgiveness finally settled in and I made myself accept what had happened and allowed him to move back in.

My boss at the law firm was an attorney for the NRA, and as time went on, my duties went well beyond clerical work. I was even carrying out investigations.

You might say I'd really settled into being his "Girl Friday," but Angelo was demanding that I quit and become a full-time mom. By that time he had a good job and was making plenty of money to support us. I was back in love with him and wanted to do the right thing, so I told my boss I was going to quit. He offered me two dollars an hour more and said he would pay for me to go to law school if I would stay, but I couldn't. A few years ago I found him on Facebook and posted a message saying I should have taken him up on his offer.

At last it looked like my yearning for a real family life, like the ones you see on TV shows, was about to come true. Angelo bought a house in what appeared to be a nice neighborhood in Gardena, California. Anybody who knows that section of LA knows that there are four blocks of nice neighborhood and four blocks of "hood." But we didn't know that, so we wound up with a half-million-dollar house right in the middle of the hood.

CHAPTER TWELVE

I can't say Angelo was a bad husband after we reconciled. In fact, he became an absolutely wonderful husband, and that's what made "the big boom" even more painful. It would have been easier if he'd been abusive or mean up to that point, but he wasn't. I was living what I considered to be a typical family life.

Flashbacks from my early years still lurked in the recesses of my memory even though I'd been seeing the same doctor for ten years for my PTSD. The traumas I'd endured came back to haunt me in nightmares and night terrors. Much later I discovered the doctor I'd trusted to make things better had messed me up instead. He kept prescribing more and more drugs during those years, saying it would help the PTSD. These days I see way too much overmedication of vets and other PTSD patients I talk with and counsel. There is much more to working through PTSD than numbing yourself with drugs.

Despite my difficulty in retaining things I learned in school, I managed to homeschool my own children for five years. However, when it came to teaching them math, I found it impossible because I simply couldn't organize numbers.

When Rosemary was two years old, I became pregnant with twins. We hadn't intended to have any more kids. But much to our surprise, one slip and we made two more little girls.

I do have many good memories of Angelo even though because of him my life became such a horror later. For one thing, he was very smart. He taught me all about computers before they became the rage and talked about everything that would be accomplished with them in the future. Most of what he said came true. He could write computer code and artificial intelligence backward and forward.

Angelo never went to school for computers. I know he went to MIT briefly, but I don't believe he ever had special training. My husband simply had one of those minds that visualized what had to be done and he did it. That's why I've always been amazed that someone so smart could be so stupid when it came to common sense.

Anyway, Angelo had visions. He was a great believer in tarot cards, and often took what they said and applied it to business. For example, one day he told me he knew his future was with the telephone company. He walked into their building dressed in a suit and armed with all of this knowledge about computers. Well, his vision was right. He walked out with a job that started at fifty-four grand a year.

Angelo managed the 611 office in Hollywood. Six-one-one is the universally recognized number for telephone customer service in the United States. He was the main developer of software they used for their website and for employee interaction, and trained all the presidents and vice presidents on his software applications. He routinely received "Above and Beyond the Call of Duty" awards. I was so proud of him that I showed off his awards off at every opportunity.

As a way to give himself some job security, when he wrote the code for all of the company's programs, he made sure to hide some secret gateways that would allow him to hack back into the system if they tried to fuck with him.

During that period of time I was very active in my church and went around and spoke at other churches. Angelo went to services with me and the kids. We went out to eat, did housework and went to the beach together. We were exactly what I'd always dreamed of—a family just like the one in the old "Father Knows Best" TV show. Even my PTSD was sort of under control. I'd rarely known this kind happiness in my life.

However, all of the childhood physical abuse was finally catching up to me. I suffered from back problems. A disc finally ruptured and after that it got harder for me to do things. We enrolled the girls in public school and right around that time Angelo began to do some work in the music industry. At first I didn't want to admit what was happening, but eventually the time came when I realized I'd lost him.

If there was anything I knew it was the music business. While running the clubs I'd had so many experiences with the dirty side of the business I was certain no good would come of his new passion. Back then I couldn't explain the evil, or the kind of people who were behind this underworld that ultimately destroyed lives like they were nothing, and they loved to recruit talented guys like Angelo. It took a long time for me to recognize that it was the Illuminati, whose power is said to lie in the occult and in the economy. They touch many people in the entertainment business with their philosophy that money creates power. I knew it was bad—forces that could suck you down like a whirlpool—but I didn't grasp the extent of their power and that they really were after Angelo.

As time passed, the physical pain from the ruptured disc brought back body memories. My health problems and PTSD were getting worse. Body memory is not like mental memory. The body remembers hurt and injury subliminally, but you aren't aware of them consciously. Finally I couldn't take the intense pain anymore and had to go in for back surgery.

Sometimes we think we want to know what's going on in our lives, but down deep we don't really want to find out. And that's where I was in my relationship with Angelo. On our wedding anniversary a friend and I went to a tattoo parlor. I came home with a tattoo under my belly button that said "Angelo." I wanted to show him how much I loved him and I guess it was also a test to make sure our relationship was finally on solid ground.

That night I expected to see a big smile and pride on his face when I showed him what I'd done. Instead, he took one look at it and became furious. "Why the Hell did you do a dumb thing like that?" he shouted.

My immediate reaction to his tirade was that maybe he was having another affair. Guilt and knowing you have something to hide can certainly trigger anger. Looking back, I wish an affair was all it was.

The war I fought at the end to hold onto my family life was the biggest one of all, and it's a fearful subject for me to go into. The physical and emotional pain was making my PTSD hard to deal with, and the doctors medicated me so much that I really felt crappy. Worse yet, it seemed that everything was unraveling and thoughts of suicide crept back into my soul in bits and pieces. I was ravaged by insecurity and things I didn't understand. I'd shut my emotions off for so many years just to survive, and now that my marriage was tumbling, I was learning what it was like to feel all of the hurt and pain. It was so unbearable, it tore me into pieces.

My only salvation was my overflowing love for God, for everyone, and especially for my babies. I always said they were the only things I did right. My poor little Munchkins. My Baby Bellas. That's what we women in La Bella Mafia call our daughters.

When I went into the hospital for back surgery, Angelo came to visit, but he always seemed angry. Not only that but he was constantly sweating and showing other signs that he might be on drugs. Maybe cocaine. I'd been through enough of it myself to recognize the signs in a heartbeat.

He'd bring me Starbuck's and push my wheelchair to his new BMW, anxious for me to hear the most recent house track he was playing in the clubs. He was so clueless. Anybody who knew him said he was an out-of-this-world genius. Yet here he was, getting sucked in like a babe in the woods. While he sought my approval for the soundtracks and brought occasional treats, his whole demeanor toward me was changing and emotionally he'd turned cold as a glacier.

After I was released from the hospital I had to go into another facility for a couple weeks so they could wean me off the hard pain meds that had me all messed up. Finally the day came when I was able to go home again. Although I was still in a wheelchair, I felt better. I put on my wedding band to surprise Angelo. Oh, he was surprised when he saw that, alright. And boy was he pissed.

I wheeled over to sit by him and he took one look at the wedding band, stood up and pulled back his foot and kicked me hard in the exact spot where I'd just had back surgery. It was as though ragged shards of glass had been plunged into my back, and I gasped in pain.

It wasn't until much later I learned I wasn't the only victim of his violence. While I'd been in the hospital he'd beaten Marie. He told her he was going to do the same to me until I stopped breathing, and she and Rosemary would be left with nothing.

Even without that additional knowledge, I'd just been hit with a double whammy. The two men I loved so much both hurt my back in the same place. I was freaking out and scared and angry. Angelo had never hit me before. Weakened by the blow, I struggled through the excruciating pain and picked up the phone, then fixed him with an icy glare. "It's the police or it's the front door."

While I sat there trying to get up, he ran into the other room and grabbed his computer, his book and a few clothes. I guess he forgot about the three boxes he was hiding in the garage, but we'll get to that later.

After he left, reality set in. What the hell was I going to do now? Instead of feeling more secure, I was in the most vulnerable position I could possibly be in and my heart was crushed to the core.

With Angelo gone, my mom came over after work most days, but that wasn't until midnight to two in the morning. She helped me get back on my feet, or at least enough to the point where I could stand up and fight.

There was money in the bank account when Angelo first left. Then all deposits stopped. When nothing was left I had to shut down our joint account. He had literally disappeared, and I didn't have a clue where he was. In fact, I didn't know if he was dead or alive.

The mortgage on the house in Gardena was $3,000 a month, and that didn't include all the other bills. There I was, alone with four young daughters, and the park ten feet from our house had gangs of Crips from surrounding towns like Long Beach and Compton playing ball or watching games on the little portable televisions they brought with them. They drank their forty-ounce beers and smoked their "blunts" (hollowed out cigars filled with marijuana). It was obvious that all of them were real curious about the lady and little girls in the house next to the park. I'd thought my life couldn't get any worse, but my household became the focus of their attention.

Now I not only needed money, but I needed help because I felt my family was threatened. It might seem that the natural thing would have been to call Angelo. After all, his little daughters appeared to be in physical danger and we barely had enough money for food. But it wasn't like I could call Angelo at work and tell him about any of it. Because of the nature of his job, his whereabouts at the telephone company were protected and it took a special security number to reach him. As a further precaution, that number was changed constantly. There was no way for me to even confirm if he still worked at the phone company.

Well, I've always been a survivor and this time was no exception. The first priority for me was to figure out how to get my kids fed. I applied for welfare and domestic abuse assistance and got it. The $900 a month wouldn't even cover a third of the mortgage, but it was something. I stood in food lines at homeless shelters and churches to get my daughters something to eat. A far cry from my glamorous days working the clubs on the Strip.

Maybe the word about our plight was out in the neighborhood, because I remember one night somebody put groceries on our front porch and I never did find out who it was. I was traumatized big time and it was amazing I was able to function at all.

Somehow, some way, a loan came through every month until I sold the house, but it took two years. All the while I was struggling to survive and provide for my girls, and we were being closely watched by the hood.

At last Mama Bear and the Gangster Girl I used to be were back. I got my mind in gear and it was as though autopilot came on. It was time to break out of my fear, get creative and use my survival skills.

Don't think that was easy because it wasn't! My heart was shattered beyond repair and I was so scared that I shook and cried every night. Anyone who says you can't die from a broken heart is full of it. Night after night I felt as though it might be my last one on earth. I kept the lights in the house off and watched out my window, trying to memorize all of the people who came to the park on a regular basis. To play their game I had to know who seemed to be the top dogs, and who did what, when and where. So I memorized it all.

Some people really find their greatest strengths when pushed to the wall in order to survive. That was me. Here is where we come to the part about a white girl becoming a boss to the Crips. Instinctively I knew the key was to make them all hood famous—known and respected. To do that, I had to join them and develop a real solid relationship with each and every member. The boys in the hood had big dreams and I took what I knew about the music business and what you had to do to make it as an artist and put my knowledge and contacts to use while managing to hold onto my sanity.

When I was in Hollywood I'd met a lot of the big rappers. Many of the wannabe rappers who performed in the hood had actually gotten some gigs in Hollywood. They gathered on this one corner near my house in front of a liquor store.

I'd begun to work with a rapper named Estefan who had a studio close to my house. Estefan was a Blood and a member of the Puerto Rican Mafia, with a reputation as a dangerous guy. Crips are publicly known to have an intense and bitter rivalry with the Bloods, so naturally the Crips in my hood didn't really like him, but they feared him and therefore treated him with respect. Since I was already in gangster mode, working with Estefan enhanced my image as one tough cookie.

Many of the wannabes assumed that because of my relationship with Estefan and what I'd done in my past life, I'd be interested in managing rappers. Pretty soon a parade of Hummers lined up outside my house to drop off their CDs. A few of them were managed by Estefan but wanted me to handle them instead. When they'd come over to my house all high to make their pitch, I just played along.

In the eyes of the guys in the hood, I was becoming a force and they started looking at me as a "homie." One by one I made it my business to meet each Crip leader, because I knew without doubt that was the key was to make them "my boys." Through me they became well-known, and in their world that equaled fame and earned me their highest regard.

On Sundays, the Crips came down and we had "music-offs." Me and my hood girls brought our own weed and had the best music, and that's what kept us at the top of the heap. At first the girls used me to try to gain their own roles of importance, and when that didn't work they left out of jealousy. However, without me they found they couldn't even drive through the neighborhood without being harassed and eventually came back into my camp.

Through all of this I blocked out the intense pain and most of the emotion. I went to church constantly where I cried my guts out on the floor. I begged God to get me through because I didn't understand how he could allow something like this to happen after all I'd already endured.

For nearly a year I poured everything I had into earning my stripes in the hood. I still didn't know if Angelo was living or dead, so keeping my girls safe was strictly up to me that entire time. I'd fought hard to earn my credibility with the Crips and waged a daily battle to keep my new reputation intact. I drank gin because gin makes you crazy, and in the hood crazy equals respect. I stayed away from the crack and every other drug the others were on. I knew if I touched that stuff and kept touching it, they would control me and not the other way around.

There were a lot of battles of the mind and a few broken bones. I was raped in the middle of the park by one of the homies, but when I told my Crip friends they administered "hood" justice. Bella was back and nobody was going to run over me ever again and get away with it.

Money was still a huge problem. Each day when everyone had left the park my daughters and I collected cans and bottles to get the rebates. We always managed to make it cool, though. Even in the worst of times I tried to make them laugh. Their world had been turned upside down and they deserved as many lighthearted moments as I could provide.

I continued trying to find Angelo. In desperation one day I called one of the 611 offices and pleaded my case to the dispatcher.

I said, "Angelo, who would be your boss, is my husband and I haven't seen or heard from him for over a year. He left me flat, my house is going into foreclosure, my kids are hungry and I just don't know what else to do." I began to cry and said I didn't even know if he was still alive.

She said, "Well, I'll pass on the message."

Shortly afterward I received a call from the security supervisor and he lectured me about what I had done.

I was nice and said I understood it might not have been right, but what other options did I have? I told him everything. I even told him about the night we only had enough money to buy four cookies as dinner for me and my four daughters.

He must have taken pity on me because at last he said, "It's against regulations for me to tell you where your husband is, but he's alright. Have you thought about filing a missing person's report? If you haven't, you should."

I thanked him, but then he surprised me by adding, "Do you think your husband might be on drugs?"

"I'm not sure why you've asked me, but yes, I do believe that he is."

"Well, I probably shouldn't be telling you this, but because of the strategic position he holds, we can't just fire him. However, we've suspected drugs and I'm going to investigate further. You see, if he is on drugs that could result in a security breach."

Okay, I'd found out what I needed to know. I wasn't sure how, but I was determined to track Angelo down and teach him a lesson. He'd learn that when he messed with me

La Bella Mafia
he'd messed with the wrong girl.

CHAPTER THIRTEEN

I was acquainted with a guy named Paulie from a part of LA called the Jungles. It was a place you wouldn't have heard of unless you were from there. If the unwary were to enter the Jungles, few would make it out alive.

Paulie was a sharp dresser and drove a nice car. He made his money establishing businesses under the DBAs of members of the Hood. The Hood members could claim legitimate business ties, but Paulie ran and benefited from everything, including cleaning services and ATM machines. Later, when I was forced to apply for SSDI (supplemental security income/disability), I discovered I was a business owner in one of the ventures. In this dog-eat-dog world I, in turn, used Paulie to my advantage. Having a dashing and successful businessman visiting my house at regular intervals impressed the Crips and made me appear well-connected.

From my days of organizing clubs, I had vision and knew how to write business plans. However, because of my PTSD, I sometimes went into blackouts and didn't remember creating them. Anyone who has ever suffered with PTSD knows this isn't unusual.

My friends in the Hood will always have my heart—

they fed my kids when they were hungry, watched them and made sure they were safe. There were only two white families on my block. Around the corner was a good woman who threw my butt in the shower and fed me when I broke out in fevers. The other couple wasn't at all nice. When Angelo and I first moved in—over ten years earlier—we smoked some weed with them, but things changed.

Toward the end, and I have to say this is funny, the wife stalked my house and tried to get her nose into my garage—as though I had something illegal going on in there.

Her husband later accused me of being on speed. Well, I wasn't on drugs then, so that was kind of funny, too. But the most bizarre thing was when they accused me of being the drug lord for all the gangs in the area.

Until then, I knew I'd played my role of the tough broad no one owned very well, but being accused of being the drug lord was like getting an Oscar! When that happened, I did have to report them to the police department. I said they were profiling me because my friends were black. Ironically, a black female cop showed up and took the complaint.

After Angelo had been gone about a year, he finally sent me an e-mail. I'd learned he was under investigation at the telephone company based on the information I had given them. He was collecting disability on some bogus claim and never showed up for work. Angelo told me he was part of an identity theft ring and that's why he had to go underground.

After the e-mail he phoned me and wanted me to come meet him where he was hiding out. I had been through so much hell I really didn't want to subject myself to him again. I sprawled on my bed and prayed for an answer. I loved God so much that my values compelled me to finally agree to the meeting.

I drove to the address Angelo had given me in the Hollywood Hills. When I pulled into the driveway, I was surprised to see at least ten security cameras facing in every direction. What the hell had he gotten himself into now? I knew some of those big estates had tight security, but this was overkill.

When Angelo opened the door, I was shocked. In the year since I'd seen him, he had lost so much weight I felt like I was looking at a scrawny, wet rat. I followed him inside, and what I saw awakened memories of the past. My father could very well have lived there. The place was filled with eye-catching stuff, including a pool table and video games. He led me through a big kitchen and then into the living room where the images on the big screen TV comprised a montage of shots from all of the security cameras.

I walked up to a framed poster on the wall on that read "Frankie's Rules." I said, "What the fuck? Who's this fucking Frankie guy? Did you become a fag on me? Frankie's Rules? I've never known you to call a man Frankie before."

He didn't answer my questions, and only said, "I'm not the same guy anymore."

We sat on one of the sofas and Angelo began talking crazy, saying that there were demons in the house and he had demon bites on his legs. He pulled up one of his pant legs to show me the marks. To me, they actually looked like a staph infection. It didn't take a genius to figure out that something was really off. I was getting so tense that I reached into my purse and took some muscle relaxers.

Angelo took my hand and led me to another room. He said, "If you sit here long enough, maybe you'll see the demons yourself." After a few minutes without any demons appearing, he walked me into his bedroom. My initial thought was uh-uh, we're not doing this. But that wasn't what it was about.

His closet door was open and I got an eerie feeling when I saw the neatly hanging garments. He'd bought the exact same clothes he had worn when we were together.

He motioned me to sit on the bed and he positioned

himself with his back to the surveillance camera inside the room. Then what he mouthed haunts me to this day.

His lips formed the words, "Help me. Help me." I saw genuine fear on his face as his eyes darted back and forth. I was about to ask what was going on when he put his finger to his lips. The message was clear, "Shut up! Don't say a word!"

Everything seemed so surreal, almost as though I was watching a thriller.

Although I no longer felt the love I'd once had, I was concerned for the tragic figure he'd become and very fearful for his safety. Whatever he'd gotten himself into, I was now sure his life could be in danger. We sat there in silence for a few moments while his eyes confirmed my thoughts.

He finally broke the silence and got up from the bed. "You should probably go home now." Reaching into his pocket he withdrew a roll of bills, peeled off a twenty and handed it to me.

That bastard! He had a whole pocketful of cash. I was still struggling to make it through every day, and he gives me a twenty? I couldn't get out of there fast enough.

When I got home I discovered that my daughter had found the number I'd jotted down on the pad by the phone when Angelo called me. She dialed it and left a message that she was trying to reach her father. While I'd been gone, Frankie had returned the call and left a message on my machine never to call that number again.

The next day I got a collect call from Angelo. Just when I thought things couldn't get any worse, he said he had threatened one of Frankie's neighbors with a knife and was in jail on felony charges. I knew he had a phobia about jail. My first instinct was to say, "Go to hell," but I couldn't find it in my heart to do that. I decided to give him one more chance and do what I could to help him.

I called my friend Tessa, who was then working as a Public Defender at the courthouse. Just moments before court convened she was able to arrange for Angelo to avoid serving the ninety-day sentence he was facing. Tessa made it a point to tell me she did it because she loved me, not for him. I thanked her and said I'd only ask a favor like that from her once. This was his one-and-only chance.

I'd put myself on the line for this stupid ass, and what did he do? He gave me a phone number that turned out to be a girl he knew named Honey. When I called her she told me he had beaten and raped her, then drugged her in an attempt to use her in a snuff film. Somehow she had managed to escape. She said Angelo and Frankie were selling drugs and importing women from other countries to use in porn and snuff films that were shot at Frankie's house. She claimed that until recently she'd had no idea he was married with four kids.

I asked if she knew why Angelo looked so awful. She explained he was so addicted to cocaine he barely left his room anymore.

I didn't know how credible Honey's story was. But considering my personal observations, I couldn't just dismiss it. And if what she said was true, things were worse than terrible.

My head was throbbing from the horror of everything I'd learned in those few days. I couldn't stand the thought that more might be lurking in the shadowy life my husband now led.

CHAPTER FOURTEEN

As I look back on it now, nothing prepared me for what came next. Many of us have experienced something called a "waking nightmare," but mine turned out to be real.

My father had always been a guy no one wanted to tangle with and I was determined to take over his legacy. From the time he died I wore his ring and swore I would never take it off. Somehow, looking at it and feeling the heft of its weight on my finger gave me the strength to go on, even when I thought I couldn't.

As I became a tough member of the Hood, my mother became very concerned for my safety. One day she came over to have a heart-to-heart talk with me.

"Bella, I look at you and I see your father." She grabbed my hand and tried to take the ring off. "Take this thing off and stop running with these gangsters."

I looked into her eyes. "Mom, it's dangerous for you to come over here like this. You're walking right into the path of the Hood wars. You just don't understand what I have to do to survive until I can sell this house. I can't go into all of it now, but it's really not safe for you to come here. Once we're out of harm's way, I'll tell you everything."

Fear radiated from her like a living thing. However, her voice remained level despite the fact that it shook. "Bella, take—off—the—ring."

"Sorry, Mom. The only way it comes off is if you cut off my finger. This is my strength!"

She didn't ask me again.

Not long before I was finally able to sell the house I discovered three boxes shoved deep in a hiding place under the garage. I pulled them out and as I carried them into the house wondered what could possibly be inside. I rationalized that maybe they were just some personal papers Angelo forgot when I kicked him out. I set the boxes on the kitchen table, and as I opened the first one I realized my hands were trembling slightly.

Inside were newspaper articles about Angelo's best friend being an alleged mobster, letters from him and pictures from prison, and unedited video tapes that showed deviant sex acts being committed. There were also contracts on people's lives and detailed accounts of rapes and tortures that another of his friends liked to perform. In addition, the boxes contained a few books that Angelo wrote and, of all things, some children's novels his gangster friend had written.

Page by page, tape by tape, the horrible reality of my husband's secret life unfolded, each page and tape worse than the one before. I remember thinking Frankie was surely part of this crime ring as well, if not the actual driving force. There was no question in my mind that Angelo would try to retrieve these boxes. Considering the contents, he'd have no choice. And if I was there when he came for them, I knew he'd do anything necessary to get them from me.

All kinds of crazy, violent thoughts flashed through my mind. I recalled what Honey said about the men bringing girls in to make sex films and that Angelo had talked to her about snuff films. There was no denying that everything spread out on the table before me confirmed her story.

I was PISSED!!! When I said my nightmare was real, I wasn't kidding. By then I was so angry at the world, when one of my neighbors came over I grabbed the beer he was holding and smashed it against the wall. I felt bad about it later, but my anger was boiling over and I simply couldn't hold it in anymore.

There was a whole lifetime's worth of angelic art statues and other artifacts worth thousands of dollars stored in the garage. In my rage I was angry with God for letting this happen when I'd loved him all my life. At the end of my rope, I went into the garage and one by one grabbed every statue and artifact and smashed them on the floor. I was certain God hated me and this was my punishment.

When I calmed down I took the boxes to the Gardena Police Department. At first they wanted me to just make a report at the window. When I wouldn't go for that and raised my voice, they took me into an interview room and taped my whole story with the evidence sitting on the table. But many times during the interview the officers snickered as though they were sharing some private joke. And their body language and the glances they exchanged made it clear to me they thought I was a nut case.

I believed I had brought them overwhelming evidence of kinky and illegal activities, but to my surprise they didn't want anything to do with me or the incriminating documents and tapes. They looked at some of the papers and copied a few. But they didn't watch any of the videos. I was stunned when they told me to pack up my boxes, the interview was over.

Their explanation was that these were Federal offenses, and I'd have to take them to the Feds. Here I was, a terrified citizen reporting serious crimes, and they brushed me off, literally kicking the can down the road. I remember thinking, "If law enforcement isn't the least bit interested in this, then what?"

On TV the police protect people like me—a frightened woman with four little girls and boxes full of incriminating evidence. As a last resort I'd broken down and begged the police to do something. Put me and my girls in a safe house, or whatever you see them do on TV to protect witnesses in danger. They did nothing.

Gangster girl was on her own again.

After my experience with the Gardena police I wasn't about to get the same treatment from the Feds. I was truly at a point where I didn't know what to do, so I hid the boxes in the house while I tried to figure out my next moves. But one thing I knew for sure—those boxes together with what I'd seen at Frankie's house meant I was in real danger.

Not long after that Angelo wrote me a letter with a line that sent chills down my spine. "I am going to carve 'bitch' in your body and that's just the beginning." As I read those words over again and again, I fingered my father's ring, craving the strength it gave me to go on.

It was the first of many letters, but from the time I read it I knew my worst fears had come true—the day would come when he'd finally get to me. I couldn't let my fear take control, though. And it wasn't just for me that I had to stay strong. It was for the safety of my four innocent little baby Bellas.

I recall one night when there was absolutely no doubt that Angelo was stalking me. I asked a woman from the Hood, who spent a lot of time with me, to watch the girls while I went to the police department and demanded help. I told the cops I could see and hear Angelo outside my house and he had no business being there. It had to be obvious to them that I was terrified. But once again the cops made me out to be crazy. Who knows? Maybe I looked and acted pretty wild, but that's what intense fear will do. I'm sure the terror I felt and the reaction of the police was just what Angelo wanted and hoped for.

The cops assigned a detective named Dick to handle my complaint. I secretly called him "Detective Dick Fuck." We yelled back and forth at each other like some married couple.

Dick Fuck screwed up his face until it turned red and shouted, "This is a typical domestic dispute, not a crime. Oh, we can take some precautions just to make sure it doesn't turn into another OJ case, but it's nothing more than domestic—not criminal, hear me? Go home."

I was frustrated and scared at the same time. But frankly, more than that, I was furious. I was living on the edge and when Dick Fuck said that, I transitioned into complete fight mode. My PTSD was in full effect. In my mind I was a warrior fighting a war! How could they call this "typical" by any stretch of the imagination?

I told him about Frankie and repeated everything one more time at a very slow pace, hoping I would somehow break through to this uninterested cop. I showed him the written threats I was now receiving on a regular basis. "Don't you understand what I'm trying to tell you? This is not a typical man, and this is anything but a typical dispute. My husband is a computer genius who built a whole software system for the phone company, he has mob ties, and he makes snuff films. Can't you see I'm in danger?"

It was a waste of breath. Dick Fuck had made up his mind. To him I was going through the typical domestic issues almost everybody experiences. It was obvious that his take was that I couldn't handle it very well. I just needed to calm down and realize that I was overreacting.

I reconsidered taking everything to the Feds, but I wasn't sure I could go through the whole fiasco again. If they turned me down, I knew something in me would crack and I wouldn't be able to put it back together again.

I admit that I did try a few suicide attempts during this time. One time I rationalized that people would take care of my girls and I took a whole bottle of 2 mg Klonopin, a drug to control panic attacks. I guess it wasn't my time, because I woke up at 5 am. The only effect of all of those pills was that I was groggy. I was so tired of fighting, but it didn't work and then I didn't have any more meds left. Damn, I can remember vividly what my hopelessness felt like. There are times even now I'm angry that I've been forced to live in the middle of nowhere, forced to leave everyone and everything I loved to be safe. When the anger comes, I try my best not to feel hate or self-pity. But deep inside a little voice whispers, "It was so unfair."

Toward the end of my time in the Hood I did everything I could to escape the neighborhood as quickly as possible. I knew I had to seek a place Angelo would never find me.

While I was trying to lose Angelo, I continued to watch out for others in the Crips and would hide runaways from time-to-time. At one point I hid one of the teenage boys from around the block and a girl as well. Then one day, out of the blue, the cops came to my house claiming they were looking for them. Thinking back, I don't recall the law enforcement team showing me a search warrant when they arrived. They just said they were looking for runaways and came right in. This was not a typical occurrence.

Who sends a team of as many as 13 "suits" and uniformed officers to look for runaways? When the under-aged girl surrendered, a woman on the team suggested placing her with social services. Then a "suit" took her to his car and within my hearing told her the raid had a larger purpose than rounding up errant kids, but did not elaborate.

Because I'd been preparing to run for my life as soon as my house was sold, everything was already in boxes spread around all of the rooms. The cops asked me when I was planning to leave. I told them as soon as the house sold. It was nothing short of a miracle I'd been able to borrow so many thousands of dollars to stay afloat as long as I had.

While everyone appeared to be there only for the sake of the runaways, a man of Italian heritage took me aside and whispered to me, "We know who your husband is, we all know. My suggestion to you is get out of here as soon as you can." And they left.

Who knows what they were looking for? I sure didn't. Maybe this was all about actually seeing if I was the drug lord they thought I was, and maybe they were looking for what was in the boxes I'd already taken to the police once. That's the weird thing. I was ready to hand them everything I had relative to Angelo, but they'd told me to take the boxes and go home. They weren't willing to take any action then, and now they were searching my house and the Italian guy lets on it's about Angelo. I guess I'll never know the real story.

Like I said, the gangster girl in me took over. First I hunted down as many of the people whose names I found in the boxes as I could. I was determined to find out what my husband was into. At that point I didn't care what gang, mafia or mob they were from, there's nothing worse than a pissed off wife with hungry kids. I actually was able to find phone numbers for many and called those numbers. No one answered, but I left very explicit messages. Maybe once I had enough information I would do just what those do-nothing cops suggested—go to the Feds. There was no way I'd be brushed off again, and I decided I needed even more evidence than what the boxes contained.

To my surprise, within 24 to 48 hours of making those calls I became aware that my phones were being tapped. Then one day a black helicopter briefly hovered right above my house. That had to be the scariest thing I'd ever been through. I couldn't believe it myself and thought maybe I actually had gone crazy from the stress. But my neighbors all saw it, too, so I knew I wasn't imagining it.

Thump thump, thump thump. This is what I heard

on and off for almost a week while that damn helicopter was hanging out in the area. Sometimes it would stay in the distance as it circled. But on occasion it would hover over my house for a couple of minutes; and that's when the noise got bad. I just wanted it away from my home and out of my neighborhood.

I remembered that Angelo had bragged and flashed the manuscript of a book he said he'd written while he lived in Boston. Supposedly it was about one of his gangster associates and had to do with a secret governmental mission he had worked on. It was his prize piece and Angelo made sure he took the manuscript when he left. Surely that wasn't what the helicopter was about, or was it?

More likely, word had gotten out about what was in the boxes even though the cops did nothing. Whatever it was, I knew I was in over my head and began to question myself and my actions. I was in survival mode and this was my reality. I was completely and utterly alone.

Angelo had claimed the Feds put a stop to the book because of how much he knew. He'd even shown me an article referring to the book in the Boston Times. Crazy! Maybe that was what the Italian cop meant when he said, "We know who your husband is."

Anyway, I never did take the boxes to the Feds and never found out what the helicopter was about. But I did try to use what was in the boxes as a road map to understand this man who was my husband. I came away convinced that I'd married some sort of monster masquerading as a loving man. It wasn't until I moved out of the Hood that I stashed some evidence with a therapist and threw the rest in a river. I only held onto a few things I thought I might be able to use for my own protection sometime in the future. As for the supposed book, I didn't give a damn about that and I still don't. It was all the other crap that turned my stomach.

Between the helicopter incident and when I sold the

house, my life evolved into an existence filled with non-stop stalking and death threats. Angelo must have found out I'd discovered the boxes and that I'd taken them to the police. He was arrested twice for stalking me and eventually entered a guilty plea, but didn't draw a jail sentence. During that entire time I never slept all the way through the night, knowing that was the time Evil was likely to strike.

You don't know how much you can get through until it actually happens. I had endured guns to my head, a crowbar to my throat, informants coming at me spitting out my life story as if they knew me. There were cops who tried to fuck me, not protect me. But wrapped into this thing I called my life there was one bright spot—a cop named George. He brought my kids coupons, candy, and movie tickets. He even gave me meds for my thyroid if I ran out. I am forever grateful to him for showing me that even during the darkest times someone will always reach out and lend a helping hand.

Sadly, the more I endured the keener my senses became. I developed an instinct that niggles at you when something just doesn't seem right, but along with it I retained a naïve hope that good people still existed in this world. That was my one soft spot that still needed to harden. I guess my desire to believe in good is what caused me do the next stupid thing.

CHAPTER FIFTEEN

A man I'd never seen before came to my door one day claiming to be a long-time friend of one of my neighbors. He was probably 40-something, of medium build, neat and well-groomed. I thought he had a kind face and there was nothing intimidating about him. He flashed a warm, disarming smile as he told me he'd heard I'd been having problems with my estranged husband and he thought he might be able to help me.

Help. That was the magic word and it was something that had been hard to come by. The police weren't exactly going all out for me, and now this total stranger was reaching out to help a fellow human being who was having difficulties. His manner and my desire to restore my belief in the goodness of people overrode my usual instincts for self-preservation and I invited him inside. Over a cup of coffee I said how much I appreciated his caring enough to call on me and asked him how he thought he could help.

He said that when he heard the stories about Angelo and me he realized that he knew Angelo from years ago back East. He always liked Angelo and was sorry to hear about our problems. He said he'd located him and suggested that we get together and try to resolve our issues. There was no guarantee everything could be worked out, but it was certainly worth a try. Angelo had agreed and now he was here to take me to the meeting.

I wanted so badly to end this nightmare that I almost immediately said, "Yes." He stood up and said, "Come on, let's go see him. And don't worry, I'll be with you and if things don't go well I'll get you right out of there and bring you home."

He grabbed my arm and escorted me outside to the blue Lincoln parked at the curb. I was in the passenger seat and he was walking around to the driver's side when I finally came to my senses. What the fuck was I doing? I didn't even know who this guy was and I'm taking off with him, leaving my daughters home not even knowing I'd left? The hell I was!

I jumped out of the car in a rage, my adrenaline surging. I screamed at him, "Get the fuck out of here and leave me alone! Do you hear me? Leave me the fuck alone!"

I'm tall and can be imposing when I'm mad, but I wasn't prepared for the effect my tirade had on him. In a split second his facial expression changed from self-assured to shock and fear. His eyes were wide and his mouth was agape. Could I be that terrifying? And then I noticed that he wasn't looking at me, but something behind me. I turned to see what it was and at just that moment the shouting began.

Over fifty Crips were headed toward this creep. The tableau was menacing as they shouted and gestured for him to leave or he'd be sorry he hadn't. It was like something straight out of a gang movie and my protectors were definitely a fear-provoking sight. I released my breath slowly. My boys had my back!

He retreated to his car, shouting, "You are going to die one day soon!"

Later I found out my neighbors had no idea who the stranger was—his story had been a complete lie that I stupidly bought into at first. Had Angelo really sent him or was he working on behalf of somebody else? I never found out. But I still wonder what was planned for me if I had gone along on that ride. Maybe my angels were watching over me that day.

I'd always felt more love deep in my heart than an average person, but that incident and everything I'd been through over the past year turned me icier than a glacier. As the months went by I became cold to the world and everything around me. Sometimes it was hard for me to soften enough to even love my own children. All of my senses and energy went into staying alive.

After the Lincoln screeched away from the curb I turned to go back into the house.

One of the Crips called out, "You okay, girl? Sure looked like something wasn't right."

"Yeah, I'll be fine." I looked at the still-gathered crowd and felt a smile light my face. "Hey, you guys, how did you know?"

"Ain't no mystery, Bella. We're always watching and know when we gotta have your back, what with all the problems you've been having with your ex. Never saw that dude before. Was this one of those times?"

I shrugged. "Yeah, one of those times. I'm gonna go in now. I think I need to be alone for a quick minute. Thanks again."

Back in the house, while I waited for the shaking to stop, I mulled over some of the threats from Angelo. The first threat he'd sent me was a duplicate of one his gangster buddy had used on someone else. So much for originality!

All this time I'd managed to stay two steps ahead of Angelo. Even though I was so mad and so scared, I never let him see me cry—even when I confronted him with Honey's disgusting details of his secret life. Her call, that time, made me realize that I really didn't know my husband and that our marriage would never be repairable.

I continued to open his e-mail threats, which were escalating in intensity, but didn't answer him. Sometimes he signed them with the names of his gangster friends. I guess that was supposed to scare me even more. For a long time I saved all of those threats hoping they would prove what I claimed—that I was in danger. Eventually I found out where he was staying, and when I opened his threat that night, I couldn't resist. I e-mailed back one word: the name of the street where he was living.

As part of the head-game he was running on me, he even faked a suicide one time, but I knew that was all bull. Maybe he thought it was a way to get me to let down my guard, but let's face it. That monster was too selfish to take his own life!

I will always hate him for hitting my kids, and leaving us high and dry after making me renounce my whole life to be that perfect wife and perfect mother. As my time in the Hood dragged on, filled with bodily harm and death threats, I actually developed a form of dementia that temporarily blocked out certain recollections. I hid my memories in a room without a door or windows. I'd experienced too much for any one woman to take, but I am such a fighter I wasn't going to roll over and die like he wanted.

Now a trigger, the writing of this book, has opened a door in that secluded room and has allowed the terribly painful memories to escape. I believe the dementia protected me from the real horror that was my life until I was ready to face them. My writings always produce a flood of tears as I tap at the computer keys, but they are healing tears that will finally allow me to put down my sword and dedicate my life to seeking normalcy within my limits and helping others by sharing what I learned and endured.

CHAPTER SIXTEEN

The end of my time in the Hood was drawing near. One day, after I'd lived in terror for so long while hoping to realize survival money by selling the house, the realtor said the magic words. Some people were actually interested in buying it. It felt like a miracle.

I'd learned something important while living in the Hood. People from areas where I'd had homes before, like Pasadena and down at the beach, aren't challenged by the same things as people who live in the various Hoods. They don't know what it's like having to pay so much money just to stay afloat in a one-bedroom apartment, where your kids can't run free because you're afraid they'll get caught in the crossfire of a Hood war or killed in a drive-by shooting. They have no clue what it's like to be stuck in a life of fear and hopelessness.

For most people in the Hood, if you don't know better, or in most cases don't have the resources, it's a world you can't escape. Common sense often goes out the window when you come to believe that every obstacle is insurmountable, and all your efforts are doomed to fail.

As I dredge up smashed down memories of a barely

endurable life while the chapters of this book unfold, I know I was absolutely out of my mind during that time and did some really stupid things—things no rationally thinking person would do.

For example, one night about two or three in the morning, I was so tired of the death threats and of being stalked, certain my life would be cut short and the end could come at any time, that I went on what could very well have been a suicide mission. I told myself someone would take care of my girls if I was killed—maybe deep down I hoped that would happen and I would at last find peace. I decided to visit a Bloods' neighborhood to see if I could find help. I had one of the neighbors come to my house to watch the girls and I drove off all alone into enemy country.

Driving around in a Crips neighborhood in the middle of the night would have been no big deal for me. After all, I knew all of them and was perceived as a Crip with power. They were my boys and they were cool. The Bloods were another story, though. Battles between the Bloods and Crips made the news just about every day. The Bloods would shoot at any unfamiliar person without discretion. And a tall white woman like me wouldn't be very hard to spot in Bloods' territory. If they didn't know me by sight, most of them knew a woman of my description was tight with the Crips.

I spotted a couple of Bloods at a gas station and pulled in. They looked at me with suspicion at first and may have thought I was setting them up, so I got right to the point: I asked them if they knew anyone who would do some work for me—a job that would involve violence and possibly murder. Was that an insane thing to do? Yes, it was. But desperate people do desperate things. And I was desperate.

The Bloods I talked with didn't seem shocked or offended. In fact, they gave me the names and phone numbers of four or five guys they said would do what I needed done for around $500. In a matter of fifteen minutes or less I was on my way back home, knowing that if my only option to deal with Angelo was violence, I could find people who would handle it for me. And although I never did anything with those names and numbers, my brainless excursion onto Bloods' turf gave me the confidence that I had an ace up my sleeve if it came to that.

I'm sure some of you wonder why I didn't try to recruit somebody from my own Hood. The answer is pretty simple. I didn't want my boys involved in using guns on Angelo and the consequences it could bring. But if some Bloods did the dirty work for pay, it would be strictly a business deal and no one I cared for would get hurt.

It wasn't plain luck that I finally sold the house, it was also knowing when to have prospective buyers come to take a look. And the one thing I knew about that house was when to show it. I would only allow the realtor to bring people by on weekdays and most Saturdays. But never at night because nights and Sundays were when the "little Crippers" were all out playing. Believe me, Sunday was the big gathering day mere feet away from the house. Crips were everywhere and that probably would have scared away most potential buyers.

The reason I said it felt like a miracle when at last some people were serious about buying my house, is because it happened just as housing sales took a big dive. Maybe angels were sitting on my shoulder that time, too. I'll never know. All I know is that when the house was shown I always faked being happy living there to impress whoever looked at it.

The realtor had gotten used to my saying with a tear in my eye, "It breaks my heart to have to sell this house. It's the greatest house in the world." We reached a sale price of just over $400,000 and made the deal. My attorney had advised me that if I published notification of the sale in the paper and Angelo didn't respond in the specified length of time, I would be able to sell the house if the Judge signed off. But much later when we were divorced, he was awarded $20,000, although I didn't think he should have gotten anything after all he put me through. In a way I felt badly for the people who finally bought it, but I didn't allow myself to dwell on that for long.

By the time I finished paying off the mortgage, all the caring friends who had helped me through the past two years, and some big attorney's fees, I still cleared enough to start a new and safe life.

When escrow closed I had two options. The first was to stay with my aunt in San Bernardino. She had a very roomy family house with a pool the girls would have loved. Realistically, though, that wasn't a viable choice because it was too close to Angelo and his gangster friends. The threats had escalated and I'd only be moving closer to the danger.

My other alternative was moving to the middle of nowhere, where I couldn't be found easily, if at all. My mom, now sober and drug-free, knew that I was in flight mode and stepped in. In my state of mind, her mission was to get things organized and see me through.

She assumed the role that many mothers do—protecting their young. I remember her voice of reason as I struggled to figure out the rest of my life.

"Bella, I'm going to tell you something and I want you to listen with a clear head. A week or so before your father died, he called me."

"What? Why would he do that after not speaking to you for…"

"For ten years. We hadn't spoken for ten years, but it was as though he had some premonition that he wouldn't be around to protect you. He only said a few words. 'You have to take care of Bella.' I didn't understand his reasoning then. He was the one with the muscle, but it became all too obvious a short time later. So, that's what I'm doing now. I'm taking care of you."

"But, I don't…"

"Were you going to say you don't want to leave California? If you were, face it. It is the only option. We'll get you and the girls to a safe place. This is one time I must insist you listen to your mother and I'll help you make it happen."

I knew she was right. The thought of me and my girls in hiding was terrifying, but not as terrifying as being within the clutches of Angelo and his buddies.

With my mother's help, the remote town that was to be my new home was soon chosen and the arrangements were completed. After escrow closed, I could have spent one more day in that house that had literally been my jail for too long. But—and I kid you not—as I sat quietly on my porch it felt like Satan was breathing down my neck, and I couldn't leave fast enough. It didn't take long to gather up our birth certificates, other important papers, clothes and a few personal items. I gave everything else to the Hood. And then the kids and I got into my car and I drove like a bat-out-of-Hell as we got out of there.

I drove to my grandfather's house near the Burbank airport where we stayed the night. It was a safe house in which to wait until it was time to catch our flight the next day. I'll admit that I self-medicated big time before we left for the airport. It wouldn't have taken much for me to back out because everything in me rebelled against leaving California. I was so screwed up that my mother did everything she could to keep me calm. She was afraid I'd go into fight and flight mode and get kicked off the plane. But that was a non-starter. She should have known I would be able to control myself and take care of business when I had to. This was for my babies.

I packed my last bag, kissed my mother and grandfather goodbye, and said farewell to my life in California. I left my car at the airport and made an anonymous call reporting an abandoned vehicle so it would be towed away. I bought another car when I arrived at my destination.

Leaving my whole life and my mom was the hardest and yet the best thing to do. My mother never really had a full understanding of what had actually happened to place us in such danger from a man she had once called her son-in-law, but she was there for me as she'd never been before. I know there was no way my children and I could have made such a run for safety without her help and support.

The first month in our new home everything felt so alien. I hated it and didn't even want to open my eyes. Admitting that I'd actually done it and this God-forsaken place was my future would make it too real. I took care of my girls and went through day after day in a daze until I finally forced myself to accept my new life.

However, while I was still in California and coming to grips with what was ahead, I did something that would have a major impact on my future. I went on the Internet and set up something I wanted to do after I relocated. I didn't spend a lot of time on it, just enough to lay the groundwork.

I started the online group now known as La Bella Mafia. I wanted it to be a support group for women with similar experiences as me. Initially, I limited membership to Italian women only, but eventually opened it up to non-Italians as well. I was simply known as Bella and gave out very little personal information. And then very slowly I added more abused women and a few men. They all became known as Bellas or Bellos.

During that time I called upon one of my old-time friends to help me. She called herself Bella Czech because we both have Italian and Czech in our blood. Even though we were very close, at one point she left the group, but then she came back. My Bellas always come back. We are a unique sisterhood. It makes me feel like I'm the "mom" watching over my Bellas and guiding them to a better life.

In the group we are very secretive regarding our identities and locations. Potential new members are closely screened to make sure they are who and what they claim to be. Exactly how this is done can't be disclosed for security reasons. But you can be assured that we Bellas and our friends take every precaution to protect ourselves.

For example, people think the girls and I live in Florida. We don't. Only a few very select people know where we really are, and as long as Angelo and his cohorts are alive and remain a threat that is how it has to remain.

In the eight years since its modest beginning, La Bella Mafia now counts around 200 members—and many male supporters—and offers them understanding, assistance, and most importantly, love.

PART THREE
La Bella Mafia

CHAPTER SEVENTEEN

Coming to grips with the life I'd been forced to choose for my safety and the safety of my daughters, was no easy thing.

Going from LA to a place I thought of as Hicksville was a drastic change and I didn't adapt to it very well. In fact, in the days following our arrival there I became extremely despondent. So much so that I realized I needed to throw my energy into something that would occupy my time and my mind. So I immersed myself into bringing La Bella Mafia together. It was sort of a two-way street. While organizing and helping these women I was on my own mission, trying to figure out everything that had transpired during the past several years. All the terror and chaos left me with a strong desire to make sense of my world. I'll tell you much more about La Bella Mafia, but first I need to explain the personal trauma which accompanied its growth.

I was emotionally distraught as I forced myself to deconstruct every episode, piece by piece.

As if in a war zone, I suppressed my emotions while I tried to survive in the Hood. Now it was all resurfacing, and I couldn't hide any longer.

The money that was left from selling the house after I paid off the mortgage and other loans didn't go as far as I thought it would, and was pretty well eaten up by the costs of starting all over again. My mental state was shaky at best and my physical health had suffered as a result. I just didn't feel very good but still had the presence of mind to realize that I needed counseling and a direction for my future. Foolishly, I thought the physical part could be put on hold until I brought my mind to a better place.

There were many services available through the State's Human Services Program to assist people in my position. But the process of applying for help could have qualified for battle pay. On a lighter note, I compared it to putting myself through a meat grinder. I talked with others who were in the same boat and found I wasn't the only one who felt that way. Every one of us was forced into a space that is best described as very uncomfortable. With the same determination that had served me in the past, I toughed it through to make it work for myself and my family. Overwhelmed by all the therapy and classes, I was in an emotional boot camp. Still, I managed to function and take care of my girls.

As part of the program I started therapy with a psychologist I'll call Leslie. I'd had some very bad experiences with a psychologist in Los Angeles who, in the end, wanted to use my story for his own gain. I sure didn't want a bozo like him digging around in my suppressed thoughts, and was delighted that Leslie had excellent credentials. Credentials meant a lot to me at the time.

I now understand that emotional encounters, even with professionals, are colored by their own personal experiences and baggage. I do believe she tried to help me to the best of her ability, but I didn't know that she was also coping with her own demons. Maybe that influenced the fact that she eventually demanded I choose between life and death.

From the beginning, I sat in a chair in her office and

the tears flowed. They were not the sort of tears I'd cried for my father when he died. These were different. They were about me and came from the depth of my soul. And they gushed out of me with the force of a broken water main. As the tears and memories burst forth during those sessions, I wondered if they would ever slow and eventually stop. Emotionally, I felt too small and unworthy to sit in the office chair. Leslie helped me to break through the old barriers and we began to discuss using my experiences to help others.

"Bella, you've been through so much in your life, I know you could help to save women from human trafficking. What do you say?"

She had my answer in a flash. "You mean I literally get to beat up a pimp, save a lady and get paid? I've done that for free for a long time. I'm in. What do I need to do?"

So I started my journey and signed into school to earn my advocacy degree. I was determined no matter how hard it might be for me, I was going to do it. At this point I had also begun seeing a naturopathic doctor who worked hand-in-hand with Leslie. As time went on, he actually had more influence on me than Leslie did. To this day, I call him "Dr. Dad."

Leslie had given me the guidance I needed and I took and passed the math and reading tests necessary to get into college. I scored high enough that I was able to get into psychology classes right away. As I'd suspected, school was anything but easy for me, but despite that I was able to sail through with straight "As" except for one class: computers. I had a problem understanding all the bytes and stuff, so I met with the instructor privately on Saturdays until I learned enough to squeeze by with a "C."

Funny, but it seems whenever I was in school, there was always one class I couldn't wrap my head around.

Because of my challenges from traumatic brain injury, I had to study morning, noon and night, and then some.

For every hour a normal person would study, add four to six more hours, and that's how I had to approach it. Throughout the entire education process I worked my buns off and absorbed everything I could.

I didn't allow anything to hold me down and was very passionate about earning my degree. As we moved further into psychology and other classes related to psychology, it became a little easier. I've always applied psychology to everything I've done, every survival instinct, every climb up the ladder and the way I dealt with Angelo. As they discussed various aspects of the course, I'd recognize what I'd done by acting on instinct and pin a memory to it. During that time I made many friends at school, but I was there for one thing and one thing only—to learn. Learning and therapy were my full-time job.

Meanwhile Leslie had decided she wanted to use me in a study. Later she did tell me what she was up to and had me sign a consent form, and that's when I learned she actually had begun to accumulate the data much earlier without my consent.

I'd always asked her if I had a multiple personality syndrome. I'd dealt with so many things in so many personas, I wondered if I was like the woman in the movie, "Three Faces of Eve."

Leslie actually told me she had never in all her years seen somebody weather as much as I had without having their personality split. On several occasions during our time together she said, "Working with you is harder than working with someone with nine personalities. You've literally had nine traumatic lives but you are still together and aware of everyone."

Okay, I didn't have multiple personalities. But my head wasn't the only place I was having problems. I didn't realize I'd pushed myself beyond my physical capabilities. As I continued through school my illness grew worse. My white blood count wasn't looking good. It seemed I was on the verge of leukemia. With each passing day I felt worse.

I discussed my condition with Leslie. She told me that in her opinion my worsening physical problems and the high white blood count were all due to my trauma. Her voice exuded confidence when she proclaimed, "That's why you're sick."

Leslie presented her study to a group of doctors and psychologists and made the argument that my trauma caused physical change and illness. I never saw the written results of the study because she insisted I wouldn't want to read it. In the end, Leslie turned out to be dead wrong, and toward the end of my schooling and the three years of therapy with Leslie my illness peaked.

Leslie had shared so many of her own problems and challenges with me, that by the time our sessions were over, I knew as much about her as she knew about me. Although she helped me and set me on the road to helping other women, I sometimes wonder if I didn't serve as a therapist for her as well. She told me PTSD had a time limit. She constantly spoke in contradicting statements. I may have a form of dementia as a result of the traumatic brain injury, but if I am emotionally or spiritually attached to someone or something, I'm like a dangerous computer.

When my education was completed she said, "You know, considering where you've been and what you know, plus everything you've learned now, you're like a weapon. I laughed to myself when she referred to me as a weapon. Even after all of our sessions, she obviously didn't know me very well. I was a weapon long before I walked into her office.

I believe she'd urged me to go to school because she had a vision of us working together. I know she had it all mapped out. But it wasn't going to happen on my watch.

CHAPTER EIGHTEEN

During the fearful time before I left California and went into hiding, I had actually pressed misdemeanor charges against Angelo for threatening me. I'd expected help and action, but the authorities did nothing other than continue to ask me for more and more paperwork. I was in fear for my life, so filling out the seemingly endless forms didn't seem to be the way to protect myself. Eventually I gave up and withdrew the complaint.

But just before I left, for some unknown reason the police had a change of heart. Angelo had almost gotten away with everything because they hadn't paid attention to all of the evidence I'd shown them in the beginning. And then Detective Dick Fuck and the DA's office contacted me and said they had decided they wanted to go for felony threatening, and asked if I would agree to come back to testify when the case went to court.

I'd said, "Are you kidding? If you're going for a felony conviction and think you can get it, of course I'll come back to testify."

Nine months after beginning my new life I was in therapy with Leslie and, among other things, I was working hard on building up La Bella Mafia. And then the DA's office notified me that Angelo's hearing had been scheduled and I definitely would be called to testify.

Leslie helped me deal with my dueling emotions—the elation that there might finally be some closure—and intense fear of what it might do to me to see him again in the courtroom. There was a lot of talking accompanied by rivers of tears as I sat in her office. In the end, my desire to really nail the bastard won out. You bet I'd be there!

I was all prepared to sneak into town to appear at the preliminary hearing when the DA's office contacted me again. I was told the evidence I'd provided had apparently been "misplaced," and we'd have to proceed without it. Misplaced my foot! I told them that without the evidence, all of the tapes, text messages and e-mails they had finally accepted, there was no way I'd be comfortable going forward.

When I said I didn't want to testify unless everything I'd turned over was in court with me, it was miraculously "found." Detective Dick Fuck was pretty sarcastic when he called and told me they'd located it. "Okay, so is there anything else you want so we can be sure you'll be in court?"

I said sweetly, "Not a thing. That's all I ever wanted, to be believed and for justice to be done. I'll be in California for the hearing."

* * *

After a slightly choppy takeoff, the flight smoothed out and I pushed the lever to recline my seat, closed my eyes and thought about my friend and protector Marlon, one of the Crips from the Hood. He had seen me through so much and I felt compelled to take the chance and try to see him while I was in L.A. He'd been the only guy in the Hood who didn't try to make me his girlfriend. I pictured him in my mind's eye—6'-2" and weighing in at 260 pounds or so. If most people saw him coming at them, they'd be afraid of him—very afraid—but he was a hero to me from the day I met him.

He used to pull up to my house every day in his blue Escalade and sit with me. We discovered we had a lot in common spiritually and talked endlessly about deep beliefs. Between all of my financial problems and keeping up the facade that eventually made me an important force in the Crips, having a friend like him was priceless.

As the plane winged its way to L.A., I thought about the time Marlon picked me up and said we were going to get his truck washed. It wasn't until we got there that I realized he was using me to get a free wash as part of a Ladies Day promotion. That was Marlon. When he saw I knew what he was up to, we both had a good laugh.

During those awful years after Angelo left, Marlon had gone through everything with me and always made me feel as safe as I could under the circumstances. Because we spoke about our roots and talked about how much Sicilians and African Americans had in common, I'd laugh when he'd say, "You're blacker than me at times."

I always answered, "Well, if I am black then you're Italian." I started greeting him with, "Ciao my Nigg." The next thing we knew, it became a popular saying in the neighborhood and no one but Marlon and I knew where it started.

The closer we got to L.A., the more memories flashed through my mind. Marlon was with me when I found the boxes and made the calls to those gangsters whose names I got off of some of the papers in the boxes. He was even there for me after the helicopter circled my house. We loaded the boxes in his Escalade and he took me and the boxes out of the neighborhood so we could go through them. I was so scared I shook the whole time. He just sat there as calm as could be.

Back to the present, we had landed and I scanned

the terminal looking for redheaded Geoffrey, or Geofsky as I loved to call him, my best friend in the whole world.

We were born in the same year, the Year of the Ox, and we had endless deep spiritual conversations. You know how sometimes even the best of friends get into stupid arguments that don't mean a thing the next day, but the harsh words affect the friendship? Well, I had gotten into one of those dumb tiffs with him over something I can't even remember now, and I'd held my resentment against him for about seven years.

It wasn't that he was jealous, because I was never with him. I treasured our friendship and didn't want to jeopardize it by getting into a romantic involvement, otherwise he would have been perfect. Anyway, because we thought so much of each other he really tried to patch it back together. Every couple of years he called to see if I was still mad and I'd hang up on him. It wasn't until I moved out of state that we started talking again.

He was the one person I trusted to know that I was coming to Los Angeles and why I was there and I'd asked him to meet me at the airport. When I spotted his fiery red hair, my heart leapt in joy. I ran to him and jumped into his arms. Geoffrey was about as tall as Marlon, but was very slender. Now he was back in my life—I was elated.

Geoffrey had always made life mean something to me, and I hadn't felt that in so long. I will be forever grateful that when we reunited I had over a grand in my pocket and three whole days to spend with him. We had a blast! Those days flew by and all too soon it was time for me to face Angelo.

Geoff went to the preliminary hearing with me, and that was one of the hardest things I've ever had to do. I sat by my Victim's Advocate who had been appointed to me by the court. She explained everything that would happen during the hearing and as the process moved forward, she literally held my hand when Angelo walked past me. He leaned in toward me like that was supposed to intimidate me. It didn't. But it did give my Advocate a glimpse of what I'd dealt with for so long.

After I took the stand and was sworn in, Angelo and I locked eyes like it was war. I was so angry at him, so hurt. He was more fattened up—more "Angelo-looking." The prosecutor played some of the tapes I'd provided and I identified them into evidence. I knew I wasn't supposed to talk unless asked a question, but I couldn't stop myself. I asked the DA, "You want the ones [tapes] in my lap where he said he was going to engrave bitch in my body and have me gang raped?"

When it was over, the judge upped Angelo's bail $100,000 and remanded him to jail. They cuffed him and took him away.

Call it crazy, but that had to be the most painful thing of the whole ordeal because at that moment he looked like the old Angelo, my husband. I ran out of the courtroom and the tears fell. As a result of the therapy with Leslie I had started to feel emotions, so nothing was easy anymore. I simply couldn't shut off my feelings and erect the wall like I used to.

Geoff took my arm and we left the building. He lived in the Pasadena area and my old stomping ground, Gardena, was right there by the Torrance courthouse and on his way home. On impulse I said, "Hey, come on; let's just drive through the Hood and go by the park. Maybe I'll see some of the little Crippers."

Geoff's face reflected uneasiness and fright, but he wanted to make me happy. As we drove into the parking lot he muttered, "Bella, I don't have a good feeling about this."

I laughed and said, "Don't worry. I promise everything will be okay. You'll see."

CHAPTER NINETEEN

It was obvious to me that Geoff was really uneasy as we headed for the park and wasn't exactly looking forward to meeting my Hood friends. But I kept assuring him I only wanted to see if Marlon was there.

"Geoff, please understand. Marlon holds an important a place in my heart. He loves me and he loves my kids and was there when I needed him. It wasn't because he wanted to jump into bed with me, either. It was because he's such a caring person."

That seemed to calm Geoff down a little, but his knuckles were still white as he gripped the steering wheel. We pulled into the parking lot and I got out of the car, then looked over at the house that had been like a prison for me. It seemed hard to believe I'd been gone so long already. A moment later I spotted Marlon's truck in the lot and got excited. There he was, sitting all by himself on a park bench doing one of his meditation things. I yelled to him and he looked in our direction

"Bella?"

I was still wearing the high heels and black suit I'd worn to court, and my spike heels sunk in the soft turf as I ran through the grass to him. He grabbed me, folded me in a bear hug and lifted me off the ground with one arm. I giggled when, still holding me in the air, he started rolling a blunt with the other hand. I heard his sharp intake of breath that was almost a shudder. Huge alligator tears ran down both of his cheeks.

Geoff ventured closer to us, still keeping a wary eye on Marlon. He relaxed a little, but wasn't trusting yet. Finally the three of us sat down. It was Thursday, right around noon, and the park appeared to be dead quiet.

All at once Crips streamed toward us from everywhere you could imagine: from the liquor store behind the park, out of nearby houses, from every direction they just kept coming.

Within twenty minutes, that park was full of homies. I was surrounded by a sea of blue shirts, being hugged from every direction. They all tried to talk at the same time, mostly saying they couldn't believe I was really there.

When things finally settled down, it was time for telling stories, asking questions and smoking blunts. Geoff was totally relaxed now and really enjoying himself. With his apprehension gone, the earlier expression of fear was replaced by a big smile. The guys told him that any friend of Bella's was a friend of theirs and he was welcome any time. They added, if he needed anything, all he had to do was let them know. It makes me so happy I was able to make the trip fun for him.

With all that "Cripper power" around, I felt safe. We spent a couple of hours there and, believe me, it was really hard to leave Marlon and my boys knowing that in a short time I would be going back to the middle of nowhere. I've told myself over and over again how blessed I am that Marlon is still in my life today. As the years ticked by, he moved on from the scene at the park, changed his surroundings, got his priorities straight and is well on his way to becoming the man he was meant to be. His goal is to become a truck driver and he's waiting to attend a driver training school. I can honestly say he's one person I don't know what I would have done without.

All too soon it was time for me to leave L.A. Before I got on the plane, Geoffrey and I swore never to lose contact again, and we didn't; we sent each other e-mails and talked on the phone often. But I realized something strange was happening. One day I got a really long letter from him saying he couldn't stand by and watch how I let guys treat me. My heart literally skipped a beat as I read further. He said he was in love with me and always had been. I'd never thought of him as anything other than a dear friend and didn't know what to say. We'd had a platonic relationship for so many years, that once he told me how he felt I didn't know if he could be just a friend, anymore.

After that, the tone of his letters and calls changed. He became very possessive and jealous. Unlike the person I knew and loved, he tore my friends apart in e-mail messages so brutal that I deleted them without answering them.

I guess he didn't realize that even if there was a possibility of something more than friendship between us in the future, I wasn't anywhere near ready for it then. After all, in many ways I was still fresh from the battlefield in the Hood, as well as my divorce from Angelo and everything that went with it.

A few months later, Geoff was diagnosed with cancer in his groin area. He went through surgery, chemo and every other treatment possible in a futile attempt to save his life. I stayed very close to him by phone and the internet.

A few more months went by and I got a message from Geoff's mother that he only had two weeks to live. My heart sank! I sat there with the tears pouring and made a plane reservation immediately.

When I called his mother, she said, "He's very weak, Bella, and practically in a coma."

"Put the phone to his ear. I want him to hear my voice."

She did and I said, "Hi, Baby."

At first he sounded very groggy, but then he became fully alert. There was excitement in his voice, and I heard, "Baby!"

"Yes, it's me. I'm coming to see you and I'll hug you and hug you and hug you."

His voice was almost inaudible, but I heard, "You'll have your own room and everything."

"Hey, there's no way you're going to get rid of me. You'll have six full days of me and I promise, I won't date any more jerks. I'm not going to leave your side."

He managed to laugh when he said, "Hey, that's okay."

"No, I'm serious. I promise." Unable to hold back my sorrow, I was crying quietly. We said we loved each other many times.

Finally I heard his mother's voice in the background. "Okay, let me talk to Bella now."

She said, "He has to rest. He'll be so happy to see you." Between my full-blown sobs I told her she had to be the bad guy and tell me when she thought I was tiring him out.

She told me she loved me before she hung up.

Although I packed with a broken heart, I was glad I would see him one last time. That is until I got an urgent message. Geoff wasn't going to make it through the night. His mother's message said to cancel my plane ticket. I dropped everything and cried my eyes out. Why was I losing the good people in my life now?

I remember raising my tear-stained face and shouting, "Are you serious, God? Are you really serious?"

Geoff's mother, aunt, some of his other friends and I, set up a prayer page for him on the internet, and the family shared everything that happened so I could be a part of it even though I wasn't there physically. All the time I felt as though sharp daggers were stabbing me in the heart.

Geoff's death is something that's still hard for me to grasp. It still hurts so much to know I'll never be able to talk to him again in this life, but our spirituality was parallel and I know he's happy. In many ways, he's still with me. Whenever I find myself missing him now, I think about that day in the park, how close we were and that big smile on his face. He was such a confident person, yet so humble.

Sometimes bad things rain down in clusters, and that year Geoff's death was the beginning of me losing so many people I was close to. A woman in my new home town who had become a dear friend passed away, my grandfather, my uncle, my right arm down at the center where I help, all were lost due to one cause or another. And the list kept growing until it reached twenty. I constantly questioned why I survived while all of those others didn't. Why, God? Why?

Once again I was a physical and mental mess, but despite that I kept plodding forward—doing my sessions with Leslie and pushing myself through the things that filled each day.

We'll talk about what almost killed me soon, but on a lighter side, as I continued to grow worse, my mother left California and moved in with me to help out.

She knew about my friendship with Marlon, but had never seen a photo of him. I finally showed her a picture in which there were a variety of guns and other weapons behind him.

She said, "That's Marlon? Your friend with the blue Escalade?"

I said, "Yes."

"Well, based on that picture, if I didn't know who he was I would say stay away from him. You said he is the biggest, sweetest, kindest soul, though I sure wouldn't know it from what you're showing me. So, what did you say he does, again?"

"He works with troubled kids now."

We both started laughing. The image of that mountain of a man with all those dangerous weapons behind him working with kids, presented quite a picture. It lifted my spirits and it felt wonderful to laugh like that with my mother. I love the fact that even though I didn't have a mom growing up, she was able to take this journey and help me raise my daughters. I never thought I'd get over the anger toward her that I'd held onto so fiercely for so long. But now I don't know what I would do without her. There is nothing I wouldn't do for her.

CHAPTER TWENTY

Three years into my self-imposed exile from L.A., my physical condition took a turn for the worse, and I almost lost my life yet another time.

The doctors couldn't figure out what was wrong with me. But finally the pain got so bad I ended up in the ER. The next thing I knew, they performed emergency surgery to remove my gallbladder. I was careful not to sign anything that would give them permission for additional procedures, though. If they found more I wanted to be in control of what happened to me.

One thing was crystal clear, however. Leslie's contention that all my problems were in my head was totally off-base. You see, the day I went to the ER after I'd been so sick for so long, I learned I'd actually been in danger of losing my life. During the week I was in the hospital, my doctor showed me the x-rays and explained I had a staph infection the size of a large ball. It had grown to a point where it made my right ovary grow into the wall of my uterus, requiring a complete hysterectomy.

My insurance denied the surgery the doctor said was necessary to correct the problems. That was insane because the doctors knew it was something I needed and the tests and x-rays confirmed it. I was still in acute pain and poured my heart out to Leslie.

To my astonishment, instead of being helpful and supportive, she pointed out that there was another alternative—suicide. She went so far as to say, "Bella, if you decide this is what you want to do, choose a humane way. You wouldn't want to leave your daughters with the image of you blowing your brains out."

After having guided me through so much over a three-year period, she was now suggesting I kill myself! Was she trying to shock me, or was she giving up on my therapy, having concluded that I'd be better off ending it all? This session was beyond pathetic and I felt it represented yet another betrayal in my life.

I tuned her out completely as she continued to speak. But her apparent effort to encourage me to consider suicide did accomplish a positive thing for me: I dug in my heels and took charge of what would happen to Bella Capo! Leslie and I were through.

No longer under Leslie's thumb, I searched for a medical doctor who could get me back on my feet, and I found a wonderful one. She was solidly in my corner and fought the insurance company to get the necessary treatment and procedures approved. During that time, the pain was so awful she had to give me an immense amount of pain meds and I'd go to the hospital for doses of antibiotics.

The insurance issue dragged on-and-on. Between that and the pain, I was reaching the end of my rope. By the time I'd collapsed on the floor, I'd given in and prayed for God to take me. I asked Him why He brought me through all of my trials and tribulations just to have me lie on the floor and die?

I heard him answer me. "I'll take you, if that's what you want, but if you stay and fight you'll be able to help one more…help one more…help one more."

At that moment, I knew with certainty that my mission on earth wasn't complete. I lifted my head off the floor and said aloud to Him, "You have my answer. I'll do as you ask."

With God's help I slowly and painfully managed to stand and walk to my bed. His was the path I would follow, not Leslie's.

Very soon after I made that commitment to God, many of the things I'd been praying for began to come true one after another. Among them, my insurance finally approved the many requests for treatment and I got my surgery. Right after that I found a new therapist, the same one I have to this day. He is really something special—patient, smart and kind. Everything a patient could hope for. I've had to cancel my appointments multiple times and he never charges me. So I'm sure he doesn't treat me solely for the money involved. And I have my medical marijuana license which works when all else fails to settle me down or ease pain. In my mind, it's much better than being dependent upon drugs like morphine

I only wish those who don't believe in God could have witnessed all of the good things that began happening to me. It was beyond any story or the make-believe of a movie—it was as real as real could be.

While my physical and emotional health began to improve, I slowly regained my strength and my desire to fulfill my promise to God to help others increased. Was building La Bella Mafia enough, or was there more to be done?

We never know who will enter our lives next and what influence they will have. In my case, I met a guy named Sonny who ran a business that provided counseling for people suffering from PTSD. Their "clients" were people whose problems weren't generally known to others, sometimes not even to their close friends and family. They ranged from lawyers to homeless veterans, tormented souls who you would never see enter a therapist's office. Sonny did no advertising and new clients heard about him by word-of-mouth.

Everyone has some baggage to carry in this life and Sonny had his share. In his past, he did twenty years in prison for murder. When he got out he was in an accident and lost half of his brain. He has trouble controlling his emotions and will be the first to stop traffic to pray with you in the middle of the street. Even with those problems, inside he is a very good man. Through him, many, many people have received the help they may not have gotten otherwise.

Unfortunately, if there is anything I know inside-out, it is PTSD. When I first met Sonny, there was a tugging feeling telling me I needed to help him with his work. I became very close to him and his workers and decided to join them.

Life is a trip, isn't it? Here I was relying on SSDI disability and two-and-a-half years of schooling, had La Bella Mafia up and running like never before, and on top of it I was doing what you could call underground counseling. In addition to the satisfaction that helping others brought me, I derived another benefit. While working with Sonny I met my good friend Paeton, who is my bodyguard to this day.

When I began to work with Dennis and Morgan to write this book, the emotional experience became all-consuming and draining at the same time. Dredging up ghosts that have been long buried and dealing with everything else that happened over the past year was not an easy thing to do and it took its toll on me. I found I needed some time away from doing counseling work.

I am still in touch with everyone, though, and Sonny and I always talk about working together again. However, I guess it's in the cards for us to work apart for the moment. My walk through life has been a grueling process so far. But writing the book continues to help me heal and hopefully, once my story is told, it will do the same for others who have

La Bella Mafia
endured, or are enduring, what I did.

CHAPTER TWENTY-ONE

I've learned to live with the fact that my body can literally attack itself at any time, and particularly after I've done quite a bit of writing about the past. It is mostly in the form of body memories, that sensation when your body remembers what happened to you even if your mind doesn't. Memory experts maintain that the body remembers first and I'm living proof of it.

My heart's hurting a lot this morning, which is part of the whole syndrome. When I say that these pages are soaked with my tears, it's true. For someone who couldn't cry before, now the tears flow freely. And while it may sound strange, it is wonderful that I can finally cry for myself.

Well, I'm lucky the doctor I have now, Dr. T, is a former Navy medical doctor and for many years worked with men and women who had experienced the horrors of combat. I may not have been in the military, but the wounds I suffered are ones she understands. The thing that is wonderful about Dr. T is that she not only has amazing medical knowledge and knows how to deal with my high blood pressure, migraines, PTSD and nightmares, but she also adds a very important ingredient—love.

During the last few years she has tested me in every way possible. There aren't too many honest people who tell it like it is, but that's my way. I don't sugar-coat things and sometimes during our sessions the words that come out of me are harsh or shocking. On some occasions when that happens she might say something like, "Bella, if only I could rewire you and erase some of the trauma you've made it through," and then she follows up with a hug. Other times I get on what I call a "spin." The best way to describe that is like being on drugs, without the drugs.

Dr. T and I work those episodes through, and in turn I use my experiences, feelings and training to help others who are in pain work things out.

There is always some humor in even the darkest situations. I remember one really bad day when my Mom drove me to Dr. T's office. A new nurse was in her last day of training. I was feeling sort of like a basket case when the nurse smiled sweetly. "So what is your problem today?"

"Well, my blood pressure isn't right and I have terrible migraine headaches. Also my PTSD is flaring up something awful and I've had a string of horrible nightmares."

After staring at me for a moment she said, "So, which of these is troubling you the most?"

I shrugged and said, "All of them."

The next thing I heard was, "There is a young woman here who is complaining about blood pressure, headaches, PTSD and nightmares as well."

I could hear Dr. T's answer. "Oh, that's Bella. Just show her back to my office."

The nurse looked stunned as she escorted us back.

Mom and I settled into guest chairs and pulled them up to Dr. T's desk. My voice shook a little when I murmured, "It's really been a hard week, Doc. The authors needed to verify a lot of the things we were talking about, so I asked Mom if she still had some of the newspaper articles. She said she did, but to my surprise when she came back she was carrying a whole bag full of things I thought had been destroyed long ago."

The doctor leaned forward, elbows on her desk. "Go on."

"Well, Mom asked if I wanted a cigarette. A question like that only meant whatever was in the bag might shake me up, so I shook my head, 'no.'" Then I asked, "What's in there?"

"—and?"

"And, without a word she opened the bag and pulled out Angelo's manuscript followed by many other documents I thought were part of what I threw in the river. All of this time, I never knew she had saved anything, and just seeing the manuscript and all the other papers made flashbacks begin."

Mom added quietly, "That friend of Angelo's was not a good guy. I've read the manuscript and most of the documents. He liked to dope people up on Percocet and other drugs, then break their limbs."

Doctor T's face turned bright red. She let out a gasp and put her hand on the lever for the hydraulic lift on her chair. While she twirled slightly, the chair zoomed down to its lowest position like a rocket.

Mom looked at her and asked with a straight face, "So, Doc, are you the one who's dizzy now?"

My mother and I have reached a closeness I never thought would be possible, but it wasn't an easy journey. Getting there required that both of us accept the reality of our earlier lives and gain the trust and respect for each other needed for a positive relationship. It was during that process that I came to appreciate that she, too, had gone through staggering agony.

When we opened up with each other, I learned she had many of the same issues I did, but in some cases hers were even worse. As she spoke I could see in my mind's eye how he beat and hurt her, and it broke my heart. Then, as though from another world, she said, "He was basically a good person."

Maybe in some twisted way my dad did love her and she was the woman of his life. But in his sick mind, I don't believe there was a place for what I now realize should been love.

It was then that I used my training as an advocate and the lessons I've learned in my own therapy, to help her face reality. I asked her point blank, "Well Mom, if he was good like you say, why was he hurting people?"

She breathed deeply and her eyes took on a faraway look. After a few seconds she said sincerely, "He didn't hurt his friends."

My answer had to be blunt. "Mom the truth is, yes, he did."

She wasn't ready to concede the truth and instead said, "But Bella, I got the best years from him."

I thought, "If those were the best, what could possibly be the worst?"

Clearly, helping my own mother was the most difficult counseling job I would ever take on. And I had no intention of dropping the ball, no matter how painful it might be. Over many subsequent conversations, I gradually brought her out of her fantasy world and into the light of truth.

Unfortunately, my mother's reluctance to acknowledge the type of person my father really was is typical. The abused often defend their abuser.

We can make ourselves believe what we want to, whatever is the most convenient for us. For example, I believed with all my heart that West, my ex-boyfriend who wrote for the group Guns and Roses, was just tired and had passed out in the bathroom. The reality? He was using heroin. I should have seen it and done something to help him. But sometimes it's easier for us if we don't look too deeply and risk opening up a can of worms. My mom had created a reality she could handle, even if most of it was fantasy.

Mom and I were having one of our discussions when she said, "You know, when your father started running poker games in his house, his ability to easily control people became so much more noticeable."

I thought about that, picturing how he'd have me dress up to serve cocktails at those private gambling sessions when I was only twelve years old. I had believed then that what I saw was normal—the combination of his temper, the drugs, the gambling, and watching the huge influence he had over people.

As though she read my thoughts, Mom said, "Your dad's connections with so many powerful people made him an important player in the business world, but I truly believe that escalated when he located and confronted his biological father. Do you remember when he found out he'd been adopted as a young boy and went looking for his birth father? I guess you were somewhere around sixteen then."

"I sure do. He was so happy for a while, excited when he learned who his father was. That was when I promised I would always cherish our Italian heritage and give him Italian babies. And then suddenly he stopped talking about him. I remember I couldn't understand the change in his attitude."

She hesitated a few seconds before saying, "What I'm going to tell you might help you understand. Your dad learned that his father was a highly successful businessman and was well-connected to some very influential people, some of whom were legitimate and others had questionable backgrounds. In many ways it was an example of that old saying, "Like father, like son." They were seemingly so much alike that your dad was expecting a warm welcome when he went to see his father and introduce himself. But that wasn't at all what happened. In fact, his father refused to even acknowledge him as his son and actually slammed the door in his face. It was a put down your father never got over."

As I digested her words, I felt that the rejection my father had experienced could at least partly explain his violent temper and willingness—almost eagerness—to inflict pain on the people he should have loved the most. I'll never know for sure how much that incident contributed to what my father became, but I honestly believe it played a role.

Mom and I sat there silently for a short time, both lost in our own thoughts. Then she said in a small voice, "I didn't expect to have such a deep conversation. It's good, Bella. It's good we can finally talk about these things."

Yes, it was good and I was so proud of her. A year earlier she couldn't even say his name, and now we were able to talk about him in detail. As I looked back, it was hard for me to believe how normal our "not normal" had seemed back then.

CHAPTER TWENTY-TWO

During my entire time of transition and discovery, the one thing I craved most was freedom—total freedom. Throughout my life I'd claimed no real control over guns, drugs, questionable connections and some very poor decisions. During the time Angelo was stalking me he'd also said my Mom was being stalked. She'd never been aware of the full extent of the danger we were in, but even so she was close to a nervous breakdown.

Now as I sit here filling these pages with stories I hope no other young woman or girl will ever have to experience, I know my greatest dream was to achieve the freedom to live a life that was really normal, or at least what we in this society call normal. It is finally time for me to share a poem I wrote many years ago because it reveals my inner turmoil.

THE TOWER
If there was one thing in this world I'd want,
What would it be?
The highest tower in the biggest city
Or the money it took to build it?
When I think of my tower

I think of freedom
Floating high in the air
Away from everything.
You're standing there on solid ground
Yet away from any thoughts that bring any sort of emotion
There are no clocks
You are faced with no tasks
And all dirtiness of man's creations are gone.
The sun, the moon
And the air you breathe
Is all you have
All you need
And all you crave.
Coming back down
Nothing looks the same
Even the stairs you used to climb up
Look different.
A new development of appreciation for every person and thing you pass.
Who says what the rules are?
Who really has control?
You.

CONCLUSION

When the feelings come of defeat
And my soul is feeling tampered with,
I go back to that tower.
Everyone should go.
The doors are never locked
You're never timed;
Just always remember not to look down!

CHAPTER TWENTY-THREE

"Bella Capo?" The words slid out slowly. "I—need—your help. Help me—please."

I'd agreed to try to help one of the online Bellas, we'll call her Bella Sophia, by telephone because I sensed her need was greater than what could be handled by e-mail alone.

Since I am in hiding for my own protection, very few people have the phone number I use to communicate with, or personally counsel a Bella. Before anyone is given this number we run a security check to make sure the person is who they say they are. For that reason I wasn't too concerned when I answered, even though I didn't recognize the caller's voice and the fear in it was evident. Assuming it was the call I'd been expecting, I said, "Sophia? Is that you?"

My question was answered with wracking sobs close to the point of hysteria. "Y-Yes, and I'm in so much trouble."

So began my involvement in what was a very difficult case. It took all of my skills and abilities, and those of other Bellas and friends, to guide Sophia through the serious problems she was facing. We did what needed to be done and Sophia could have been a great success for La Bella Mafia and for me, personally. But in the end it was a failure. Not because the rest of us dropped the ball, but because Sophia ultimately defeated herself by reverting to the role of victim and defending her abuser. And in the process she almost got one of my best and most influential friends into a sticky situation with the law.

Before I discuss Sophia's issues, how we dealt with them and how it ended, let me say a bit more about La Bella Mafia in general.

I previously told you about my therapist, Leslie, and how during our sessions I learned as much about her as she did about me. I remember her telling me one time, "I don't understand why when I give someone therapy, in the end they almost always become hostile toward me."

The question Leslie posed was a good one because it addressed an issue that becomes particularly apparent in the case of abused women or men and, from my own experiences in counseling. I believe there is another factor as well. Most of the Bellas I worked with were in flight mode. They had found themselves in bad—sometimes life-threatening—situations and were trying to escape. In some cases they became addicted to the run, the chase and the hide. After they were safe and okay they didn't know what to do with themselves, and had a hard time getting back to a normal lifestyle. Because I had encouraged and helped them to escape from bad relationships, they blamed me when they had trouble adapting to their new life. To complicate matters even further, some returned to their abusers. When this happens, they become angry and hostile toward the person who made them see just how dangerous their situation could become. Leslie's clients needed someone to blame and she was it.

It has become obvious to me that those in need of a lifeline don't always appreciate the person who throws them a rope. And sometimes in weak moments they will revert to defending the bad guy. How many times did I stick up for Angelo? So instances of hostility from those I tried to help were not uncommon. In fact, they were the rule and not the exception.

Getting back to Sophia, it is fair to say that many of her problems have also been experienced by other Bellas, though not to the same extent. In many respects Sophia's story is not unique to her, but applies to a large segment of our members.

I first met Sophia through the La Bella Mafia Facebook page. We e-mailed and sent private messages back and forth, but she was very distrusting and didn't want to discuss her personal situation. Instead, she said she was interested in helping others and wanted to know what role she could play in the group. After some discussion it became clear to me that she would be a valuable asset in our security operation screening potential new members. But first, Sophia's own identity had to be confirmed, and a background check run on her.

After checking her out, I got back to her and told her how she could help. She seemed grateful and excited about the opportunity. It didn't take very long for her to prove me right regarding her abilities in the security area of La Bella Mafia. But, although she was good at her job, she remained aloof—never discussing anything personal—and I didn't press her for information.

Several months passed and I sensed that she was beginning to have confidence in me because she gradually started opening up about herself. There was nothing major at first, just things like she was 50 years old, did sporadic public relations work, and had a boyfriend around the same age she was. But I knew there was a lot more to her than that and she was a troubled lady. It was just a matter of time until the dam burst. And it finally did beginning with the phone call.

"It's going to be okay," I said in a calm voice. "You're not alone. The other Bellas and I are there for you and we'll all work together to get you through whatever issues you're having."

"I hope you can help me, Bella Capo," Sophia said in a somewhat steadier voice. "But I don't know if you or anyone can help me to get my life straightened out."

"You need to believe that we can. Right now, to you, it probably seems like this is the end of the world. But I can tell you from my own experiences, and those of the other Bellas, that God's help can solve any problem. You just have to trust and believe."

"I do trust you, Bella Capo. And I want to believe. Tell me what I have to do."

"The first thing is to start at the beginning and tell me about the trouble you're in. Does it have to do with your boyfriend?"

"Yes," she said. "It's all about him. He's harassing me and threatening me. I don't know what I'm going to do."

By the time Sophia finished her sentence she was sobbing again. "Are you still seeing him? Are you living with him?"

"No. We lived together on and off while I was in New York. But when things started getting bad, I ran away to another state. Now he sends me threatening messages on the Internet sites I use and was texting me, too. I —"

"But he doesn't know where you are, does he?" I interrupted.

"No. And I've started using disposable cell phones with numbers from outside the area where I live. Now when I visit Internet sites I use a fake name and photos of other people to hide my identity."

"That's good, Sophia. What's his name? Did he physically abuse you? Emotionally abuse you? Or both?"

"His name is Vinny. He never hit me, it was all verbal."

"When did he become abusive toward you?"

"Well, at first he seemed like a perfect match for

me. We were the same age and he was very soft-spoken and gentle. But after we were together for almost a year the real Vinny came out."

"Something must have triggered that change, Sophia. Do you know what it was?"

"Yes. I know now that Vinny is a con man. He knew I owned property in a southern state that was worth a substantial amount of money. He talked about marriage and said he'd handle the property for me and I wouldn't have to worry about a thing. When I refused to sign the property over to him he got really pissed off and that's when the abuse started."

"How did you find out that he's a con man?"

"After he changed I did what I should have done to begin with—I started checking him out. I learned that he only gets involved with women who have money or assets, such as property. He charms us out of our money or other valuables and then ditches us. When a woman doesn't do what he wants her to do, he doesn't just let it go and find another victim. He takes his anger out on her instead."

I was taken somewhat aback by her admission that she had failed to do in her personal life what she was so good at in La Bella Mafia—screening out the bad apples. But that was water under the bridge. Sophia wasn't the first woman to run into a slimeball like Vinny and she wouldn't be the last. This wasn't the time for me to tell her that, although maybe I should have. I continued, "You said he threatened you. What kind of threats is he making?"

"He said he was going to scar my face and have me raped," she said, her voice breaking at the end.

"Raped and disfigured?" I said in disgust. Vinny sounded like a real sweetheart!

"I was terrified," she continued between sobs. "Every time I heard a noise at night I imagined guys dressed in black and wearing ski masks were coming for me. I feared they'd tape my mouth shut while they held me down and took turns raping me. And then they'd throw acid in my face before they left. Those thoughts had me so scared I thought maybe I should just kill myself before they got to me."

"I can appreciate your fear," I said, as I thought of similar threats I'd received from Angelo. "But you stayed strong and didn't let that fear overcome you like Vinny wanted. You didn't let him win and you can feel good about that."

Her voice was steadier when she said, "Thank you, Bella Capo. You're right, I didn't let him and his threats destroy me."

"Okay," I said. "Look, you've taken many of the right steps already, but they aren't enough. A lot more needs to be done. We're going to need to talk every day until your situation with Vinny is stabilized and then resolved. And I'll need you to be completely candid with me as we move forward. Are you up for that?"

"Yes, I am. I told you I trust you and I'm placing myself in your hands. Whatever you need me to do I'll do."

"That's the right attitude, Sophia. Understand that things are going to work out and nothing is going to happen to you. Between me, the Bellas and some big guns I know, everything is going to be alright," I assured her.

Sophia was true to her word and we talked and e-mailed regularly. Over the next few months I learned a great deal about her history. Vinny wasn't the first abuser she had dealt with. She had three children from a prior marriage and divorced the husband who had physically abused her. Since then she'd had no relationship with either him or her children.

As our sessions went on, I became convinced that Sophia has PTSD and possibly a dissociative disorder that can lead to personality issues. However, when I mentioned those concerns to her she denied having any such problems. Rather than admit to having PTSD, she said her personality and how she handles things are signs of strength.

In spite of her denials we continued to work on the most important matter: dealing with Vinny. His internet threats and attempts to locate Sophia were escalating and it became obvious that he had to be reined in. I learned through Sophia that Vinny had organized crime connections. And as luck would have it, he was acquainted with my personal friend and former associate of New York's Genovese crime family, Tony "Nap" Napoli. It might sound strange, but Tony is the person who really saved my ass and that of many Bellas with huge problems—a really good guy.

Tony and I met through a mutual friend a couple of years earlier, and when we began to talk with each other it seemed as if we'd known each other forever. We talked almost daily. It was during a two-year period that I remained in my room because I was angry and in a serious fight or flight mode. But Tony never judged me. He was another of those few men in my life who I felt was sent to me by God. He didn't put me down and always knew what I was talking about because we were from the same world.

During that time I was very deep in PTSD. But as I told Tony things about my life he kept saying, "Save that story for your book." I would get so frustrated with him when he talked about me writing a book because back then that was the last thing on my mind. But I loved him for it, anyway. Despite all of my anger and PTSD I was still helping women like Sophia through La Bella Mafia. What I had to acknowledge was that I needed help, too. It was like the counselor needed a counselor and Tony filled the gap. He gave me the strength to carry on with what I'd started.

So why did Sophia's story end badly? Because sometimes you try to help someone and they hang themselves with the very rope you throw them. Tony really showed what he was made of and how dedicated he is to helping women like us. But unfortunately, you just never know how something will turn out in spite of your best efforts. It isn't always all sunshine and smiles.

Anyway, when I told Sophia I wanted to reach out to Tony for help, she asked me not to identify Vinny to him by name. She wanted him out of her life, but didn't want anything else to happen to him. She was afraid something could be set in motion that she wouldn't be able to control.

She needn't have worried because that's not what Tony is about. But rather than try to convince her, I honored her request. When I talked with Tony I was up-front with him. I said I needed his advice on a situation in which he knew the man involved, but at the request of the woman I couldn't reveal the man's identity. Tony agreed to that condition and we began to work on a plan to resolve Sophia's Vinny issue.

For nearly a year I consulted with Tony and then advised Sophia of various things she could do to further distance herself from Vinny and eventually completely sever him from her life. Gradually, that advice paid dividends. Vinny's threats and attempts to locate Sophia tapered off and I thought we were nearing the end of what had been a very traumatic period in Sophia's life.

Then came a call from a nearly hysterical Sophia. Vinny had obtained a valid cell phone number for her and the threatening calls and texts returned with a vengeance. How in the hell did that happen? I wondered. What had gone wrong?

I later learned a woman contacted Sophia through a mutual acquaintance pretending to be a friend, but was actually a person with a crush on Vinny and was acting as his snitch. After gaining Sophia's confidence she obtained her victim's contact and social media info and gave it to her would-be boyfriend. Just as she had done with Vinny, Sophia failed to exercise due diligence before accepting this bitch as her friend.

When the new round of harassment began Sophia

was scared to the point of telling Tony the whole story. "Bella Capo," she wailed through the phone. "He found me and he's going to kill me. He said a team of men are on their way to get me right now. You've gotta tell Tony so he can stop this. If you don't I'll be dead."

I tried to calm her to no avail. "You've gotta call Tony," she demanded again. "My life depends on it."

I felt the new threats were probably another bluff, but it was obvious Sophia believed she was on borrowed time. Her panic mode, coupled with the fact that Vinny had somehow gotten her information, caused me to agree. It was time to tell Tony what was going on and who the culprit was. I uttered some final assurances that everything would be okay and then reached out to my mentor to tell him the whole story.

"Vinny who?" Tony asked. "I know lots of guys named Vinny."

I gave him Vinny's last name.

"I wish you'd have told me that a year ago," he said. "This Sophia has some money, huh?"

"Not a lot of cash. She owns some land, though, and Vinny tried to get her to let him handle selling the property for her."

Tony chuckled. "That's our boy. He hustles any broad with cash or other assets. We'll have to tell Sophia what kind of guy she got involved with."

"She already knows. After he became abusive toward her she checked him out and learned that he's a con artist. She made me promise not to give you his name or the details. Just to tell you general stuff and get your advice on how to get rid of him."

Tony was silent for a few seconds. "I understand. She's not really in any danger you know."

"I figure this guy's more talk than action. You know the guy and feel the same way, right?"

"Vinny's a wannabe tough guy. He talks-the-talk but he don't walk-the-walk. And he hangs around with other guys like himself—guys who are either have-beens or never-weres. Vinny isn't gonna hurt her or anybody else," Tony declared in a disgusted voice. "These guys like to hang around with the wise-guys hoping they'll look like they're connected. They're not mobsters, believe me."

Feeling good about how accurate my impression of Vinny had been and that Sophia was not at death's door, I said, "So what do we do now? How do we stop him?"

"I want to talk with Sophia, myself, and then I'll speak with Vinny. And that should be the end of it."

After speaking with Sophia, Tony contacted Vinny. He told me about the conversation a few days later. "Vinny denied knowing her," Tony said. "He said she must be some kind of a crazy bitch for making up a story like that."

"You don't believe that do you?"

"No, he lied to me. But that's okay. I got my point across and he knows that I know. If he's got any brains Sophia won't hear from him again."

It turned out that Vinny didn't have any brains. Shortly after Tony's talk with him, Vinny called one of his friends who published a magazine, and was also a friend of Sophia's. During that conversation Vinny implied that he was part of the Mob. To make his point he mentioned that he knew Tony. He said some things about Tony that were totally out of context, and could have been misconstrued and jeopardized Tony if heard by the wrong person.

In addition, Sophia began receiving more text messages threatening death. She was able to identify the cell phone numbers the text messages originated from and the owners of those numbers. She passed the information on to Tony.

This time Tony didn't deal with him by phone. He set up a face-to-face with Vinny, the magazine publisher and three or four of Vinny's wannabe friends. During the meeting his buddies admitted that Vinny had borrowed their cell phones to text the death threats to Sophia, and the publisher divulged the details of Vinny's call to him.

After the sit-down Tony called Sophia. He told her his opinion of her former boyfriend and that she had nothing to fear from him. He followed that up by meeting with Vinny again, this time it was just the two of them. I don't know what was said during that session, but all text messages, phone calls and social media posts to or about Sophia ceased. Whatever message Tony delivered had done the trick. It was time to celebrate a great success story for La Bella Mafia and for Tony and me personally, right? Wrong!

Tony and I knew that Vinny was an unsavory character—a con man, an abuser and a liar whose unfounded stories could have caused Tony some grief. But what came as a shock was Sophia's betrayal. That's right, the lady we had done everything we could to help turned on us. She tried to use her connection to us to further her own interests under one of her new identities. Although she didn't go back to Vinny, she no longer portrayed him as the bad guy and defended, explained away or forgave his actions.

Tony and I were disappointed, certainly. We put Vinny and Sophia out of our lives and Sophia was expelled from La Bella Mafia. What happened with Sophia was one setback among many triumphs. And we didn't let that one bad experience stop us from helping others—far from it. We learned our lesson and moved on.

Now it's time to talk about some of the victories.

CHAPTER TWENTY-FOUR

In the previous chapter I spoke about our attempt to help a Bella named Sophia, how it ended and why I considered that case a failure. I began my discussion of La Bella Mafia with the Sophia matter to show that trying to help abused women isn't always a bed of roses. Sometimes things just don't work out the way we want or hope.

Now that I've put Sophia's story in the rear view mirror I'm going to go back to the early days of La Bella Mafia to explain what we're all about and tell you some of the good things we've done—our successes, if you will.

I was in my new location, La Bella Mafia was finally running full force, and at last I knew why my life had been saved all of those times I could have died. From its very beginning I was sure this was the thing I was meant to do in life. I thought of La Bella Mafia as the essence of my mission to help others—those who had experienced the same horrible things I had. As our membership grew, my co-founder Bella Czech and I discovered that it did not matter how severe the abuse; all of the women were damaged and traumatized. We also met women who had survived worse conditions than we could ever have imagined.

I quickly learned one thing that is critically important and absolutely necessary in order to keep a Bella safe. Many of them are in real danger, so we must live by the motto, "Keep your mouth shut!" There are no exceptions.

When a woman comes to us, from the start I want to do what I do best—right the wrongs and make everything better for her. Yet I know in my heart that I can only do so much. I've also come to realize that some Bellas simply aren't ready for that phase, initially. They have a lot of anger, hate or fear inside of them that must be dealt with first.

There are always many Bellas in line who need prayer and guidance. I eagerly provide that to them with a smile on my face. And I'm not the only one anxious to help. Several other members have followed my lead and adopted my manner to counsel those in need. Caring for each other and creating a loving environment built on mutual support is the only way for our community to do what it has to.

We have made it through some unbelievable situations. What happens in the movies involves actors and actresses playing a role. They grab your heart and you feel for them—cheer them on as your eyes remain riveted on the screen. The role all of us played before being involved in La Bella Mafia was accompanied by threats, abuse and betrayal, but we weren't reading lines from a script while a director and crew hovered nearby. We really lived it and somehow survived. That doesn't mean every problem that ever plagued us magically disappeared. We deal with the tough issues—no matter how rough it gets—and don't let them destroy us.

Imagine the effort it takes to put on a positive face for others in distress when you have a multitude of stressful things going on in your own life. It isn't easy. But no matter what, my main Bellas and I keep it together. I just tell myself that everything that happens, everything we do, is part of a greater plan. Prayer is the key, but it can't happen without the support and care of others. Fortunately, I'm able to fall back on a couple of women I trust completely.

Of course, what we do depends on individual needs. First and foremost, it is vitally important to ensure that the abusers and other dangerous persons do not gain access under any circumstances to the women we protect. After it became necessary to ask Sophia to leave La Bella Mafia because of her abrupt change of attitude, we made sure that the new people assigned to security were as proficient in their performance as she had initially been.

Now I want to tell you the stories of two of our many successes. They're what give me the strength to keep going, even when I don't think I can make it through one more day.

I'll call this first story Cristella's Story, and she is truly a miracle. That isn't to say all of the tales that are part of La Bella Mafia's history are not miracles, but Cristella was in such horrible "spins" she couldn't even utter one sentence without some degree of fight. She absolutely had no control over the anger raging inside of her.

Cristella was only fifteen when we first met. I was on the beach during a visit to Florida and she approached me and asked for a cigarette. We talked and decided to stay in touch, but it wasn't until she was 21 that she turned to La Bella Mafia for counseling. That was about eight years ago. By that time, she had kept everything inside her for so long that our first objective was to let her know it was okay to finally allow herself to feel.

Cristella was like the rest of us—regardless of the degree of our traumas, we all suppressed our emotions. If we'd allowed ourselves to actually set our feelings free, we never would have survived. For Cristella, when everything began to come out, she had no control and held nothing back.

In her anger she was like a powder keg, hateful and combative. And almost anything would set her off. If she felt another person in line at a 7-Eleven looked at her the wrong way she'd say, "That bitch. I'm going to fuck her up." That was her attitude and I couldn't hold a complete conversation with her without something triggering her into hate and swearing.

During our conversations it came out that she had been molested by her grandfather when she was only four, and the molestation continued until she was twelve. He'd treated her like a little sex doll. He would shut her into different rooms where she was isolated. She talked about a hallway she called "the dark spot." She was so scared and so young she didn't understand what was going on. Her grandfather did everything to her his sick mind could conceive.

With my own background, and having been in the flight and fight mode for many years, I was able to understand what she was thinking and feeling. She knew I felt what she felt and I was able to gain her trust pretty quickly. But she trusted only me and not another soul.

She would look me in the eye and say, "Bella, you've been through similar things. You've proved yourself loyal to me in the way you opened up and shared your experiences. So many things that happened to both of us are parallel."

Cristella knew that I never judged her for what had happened. The parallels didn't stop with the sexual abuse. She had been shunned by her own family just as I was. As our bond became stronger she would tell me about the emotional abuse.

A few years after we began her counseling, someone she thought she could trust tried to kill her. She had called me while curled up in a ball in a bathroom, holding a toilet plunger as a weapon, and listening to the sounds of her would-be murderer trying to break into her house. I initiated a three-way call to 911 and the cops got to the scene in time.

After it was over I walked her back through it, so it wouldn't be buried. Within twenty-four hours I arranged for her to be on a plane and on her way to a new location where she'd be safe. She never went back.

One day as Cristella began to blossom through our

counseling sessions, I held her at arm's length and said, "To see where you were back when you were a teen, and how far you've come, fills my heart with joy. You've conquered a mountain of anger and now beauty absolutely radiates from you. The transformation is nothing short of a miracle."

She hugged me with tears in her eyes, and simply nodded.

If you ask me, God definitely has his hands on her. She is compassionate towards other people, now, because at long last she loves herself. The bubble that once surrounded her and acted as a shield nobody could penetrate is gone.

Deep in her heart Cristella was always a very loyal person, but she constantly beat herself up for what was done to her and didn't know how to make it right. Today she realizes that everything happened for a reason and she helps others with an enthusiasm that is a delight to behold. She has become a top advocate, and is my right arm and the beat of my heart.

There is no timeframe for being a Bella. When they are in trouble, whether it is now, or years from now, they need you. Period. As for Cristella, the way she has grown and overcome so many obstacles and battles, including drugs, is one of my miracles. She's clean, can hold a thought, she has clung to the love of God and is able to handle day-to-day problems.

Part of the key to bringing her into the light from the dark was her knowledge that I would be there whenever she came back to me. We still talk almost daily, but it's on a different level. Sitting here writing about Cristella, I'm beyond proud of her. She has learned enough from me and her own experiences to be able to help others. She has gone from a 21- year-old working as a cocktail waitress and doing some modeling, to being a devoted mother to her son. Is life perfect for her? That's like asking is it perfect for any of us? She still has problems, but now she is strong enough to be able to cope with them.

While every Bella's story shares some common threads, each one is also different.

Take a woman I'll call Brenda. She was a military wife who'd had no exposure to the real world and was anti-God. Anybody who approached her found her to be very aggressive and she wanted nothing to do with them. Our sessions were sporadic at first, and then became weekly.

Once we began to work together to unravel her problems, Brenda revealed that she was an alcoholic, had a cheating husband and drug-addicted parents. She admitted she had no clue what life was really all about and lived in a fantasy world. She was a typical submissive wife, emotionally battered by a husband who wasn't about to change. I was very blunt with her and said the first step that needed to be taken was to get out of that marriage.

It was as though she'd been waiting for someone to give her permission to do just that and had no problem taking direction. She filed for divorce almost immediately. With her eyes finally open to what she'd tried so desperately to ignore or justify, all she wanted to do was leave everything and run. She flew out to visit me and at that point our sessions became daily.

This was about six years ago. I worked with her day-in and day-out for weeks. She stopped drinking, went to nursing school, and out-of-the-blue found God like there was no tomorrow. Her spirituality became Number One to her. She is working and putting her life back together in a beautiful way.

Brenda has a heart of gold. When somebody needs prayer, she is on it. She spends her nights lighting candles and praying for each and every Bella. She puts them before herself. She's another lovely miracle that I couldn't be more proud of. Like Cristella, she became adept at counseling others in need. And she is only in her early thirties.

There is no age limit for our Bellas. We go from children to women in their eighties. These are the people who reach out to us and we welcome them with open arms and hearts. Their problems become our problems and we work through them together. Once they become a Bella, they know they will no longer be alone.

CHAPTER TWENTY-FIVE

As a leader of La Bella Mafia, I've had to deal with many strong personalities among our members. As a result, I have had to contend with a few power struggles along the way. I'm not going to bore you with those types of stories. Instead I'm going to give you a couple more examples of members who triumphed over their problems through team work and prayer.

Let me begin with Mary Elizabeth, who will be forever etched in my mind as one of our miracles. When she first came to us she was very withdrawn—a truly private person. And she remained so for quite some time. However, she did frequently send messages talking about God, and seemed to be a very loving person. Our initial communication was always by e-mail. But, after she had been a Bella for several months, I wanted to get to know her better so we spoke on the phone. During that and subsequent calls I learned a great deal about who she was and what she believed.

"Bella Capo," she said, "I pray all the time. I love God but my prayers have yet to be answered."

"What is it you pray for?"

"Well, I've been married several years but I've been

unable to have children. We have tried everything without luck. I have spiritual dreams that always seem like God is giving me the solutions to other people's problems, but not mine."

"Is there any medical reason that prevents you from having children?"

"No, the doctors tell me my husband and I are both healthy and should be able to have children. But for some reason I haven't been able to conceive."

Not sure of what to say, I inquired about the other messages she felt God was sending her.

"I dream about things like a wonderful man coming into one of our single Bella's lives, or about getting the answer to another Bella's family problems. Things like that."

"Have you told the people in your dreams about them?"

"No. I was a little afraid for fear they might think I was a fanatic or crazy. Truthfully, it scared me a little, too, because almost all of those dreams came true."

I felt so bad for her. She knew about the solutions for other people's problems, but her own greatest desire—to bear a child—remained unanswered.

In the days following that conversation I searched my heart for a way to help this woman who desperately wanted to be a mother. She was so gentle and loving, I knew she would be a wonderful parent. Sometimes I go to church in the middle of the night to pray for those in need. With Mary Elizabeth constantly on my mind, I began to go nightly and ask God to answer her prayers.

And then the miracle happened. After 10 years of trying and failing, Mary Elizabeth found herself pregnant. She delivered a healthy baby girl and soon became pregnant again with her second daughter! Some might say it would have happened anyway, but I say that is what the Bellas are about. Women helping women through God.

In La Bella Mafia I call many of our beautiful, talented members Warriors of God. They pray with and for those who have sunk into despair and need renewed faith. The power of prayer is truly amazing.

Sometimes expressions of hostility are actually cries for help. In the case of Rose, she had been abused mentally and emotionally by her husband and sheltered from the world like Mary Elizabeth. But rather than Mary Elizabeth's sweet nature, Rose's buried hostility drove her into a fantasy life where she pictured herself as a powerful enforcer. We recognized this and understood we were dealing with a potential firebomb.

There is one thing we know as Bellas—a person needs to deal with reality. Rose needed to recognize the world for what it is and accept where she fit in it. After that, she'd be in a much better position to confront and deal with her problems.

As with all new members, my initial communications with Rose were by emails and occasional phone calls. I and some of the other Bellas worked hard to steer her back to reality and convince her that her anger and doubt were normal for someone emerging from a fantasy life. We also tried to teach her how to be an adult who could take care of her kids, make everyday decisions and handle her own finances.

And our efforts paid off. Unfortunately, they worked a little too well, though. Rose went all the way from thinking of herself as a Terminator-type to being a character out of the Brady Bunch. She was still living a fantasy, but now it was sweet and sugary instead of poisonous. And then the reality we'd been hoping she would find kicked in and she realized that life isn't the perfect one you conjure in your mind. In her fragile mental and emotional state she lost it and actually became suicidal. In full emergency response mode we all worked together to assure her that life was worth living. Thankfully, we did, and pulled her back from the edge.

The crisis was over, at least for the time being. But Rose was still a very troubled person and the situation could deteriorate again very quickly. We all knew that if that happened, we might not be so lucky the next time. Under the circumstances, I knew that emails and phone calls were no longer sufficient. It was time for me to meet Rose face-to-face.

It is very hard for me to travel because of my kids, but my door is always open if Bellas are willing to fly out to meet me. All of us, my mother, my kids, always welcome them with open arms. When I suggested to Rose that she spend a couple of days with me she readily agreed.

When she arrived we bonded into a mother-daughter kind of relationship almost immediately, with me in the role of mentor. We took long walks around a nearby lake and talked incessantly. And when we returned to my house we sat and talked some more. I already knew Rose was an extremely unhappy person. And during those conversations I came to better understand why.

I could feel her hostility as she opened up about her miserable life. Rose's mother was only thirteen years old when Rose was born out of wedlock. Her grandparents stepped in and raised her. They were good people, but not given to show affection and they did little to educate her about life. She got married in her early teens and her husband controlled every aspect of his child bride's life. Because of that, her life experiences, the ability to cope with problems, and generally knowing how to manage herself were virtually non-existent. Now, after 14 years of marriage and two children, she was at her wits' end.

I shared my own survival story with her and told her that she was completely capable of attaining the same results I had. But in order to do that, she had to break loose from her controlling husband. She said she understood and promised to get him out of her life.

I could see a big change in Rose in the brief time she was with me. In addition to the counseling, she experienced something else she's had very little of: love. Between me, my mother and kids, she got lots of hugs, and I believe that impacted her deeply. The anger and hostility that were so evident when she arrived, gave way to warmth and friendship.

When we had a barbecue on the lawn, I received something that was alien to me as well—the atmosphere of a functional family.

After Rose left to go back home I prayed she'd find the inner strength to do what needed to be done. She did. She divorced her husband, went back to school and became a nurse.

However, there was one minor hiccup when Rose contemplated dating again after her divorce. She almost got into a bad situation with a potential beau. Based on some of the things she told us about the guy, we ran a security check on him and found out he had a record of domestic violence and drug abuse. The date never came off and Rose learned a valuable lesson in the process.

One of my personal rules is that I talk about God, but I don't force it on anyone. While I would prefer that the other Bellas turn to Him as I have, that has to be their personal decision. When Rose and I had grown very close, one day she asked me how to pray. I shared what I knew, and the rest was up to her.

I am so proud of how the hostile, naïve, Rose I first met, has turned into a confident young woman and mother, and become a professional care-giver. She now plays an important leadership role in La Bella Mafia and has become a piece of me.

That leads me to the part where I'll tell you about how La Bella Mafia works.

CHAPTER TWENTY-SIX

I'll bet you're curious about how people find us. Obviously, we don't advertise in the Yellow Pages, but word spreads through some sort of online network that we are here to help. Women—and occasionally men—interested in joining La Bella Mafia, or learning about how we operate, will attract the attention of a Bella or someone else in the know. Sometimes women's groups will post information about a rape or assault and our Bellas will contact the victims and encourage them to seek help through our Facebook page.

Now we have taken it one step further. With the publication of this book, we have established an actual blog and website for the first time since Bella Czech and I formed the group [http://labellamafiabook.wordpress.com and www.labellamafia-book.com].

As is the case in many groups, some of our members are more active than others. Thankfully, about twenty of us are especially strong advocates who are willing and able to donate our time. We share the motto: What a Bella needs is what she gets.

All of us are strong and loyal but, most importantly, we are brutally honest. As I've said previously, I'm someone who tells it like it is, and I'll state right here that we have no room for bullshit or rats. Someone caught running their mouth off or ratting, as we refer to it, is shunned and bounced from the group.

Now a few words about how the group operates. We have zero tolerance for anyone who wants to use the group for personal benefit or to spy on any of our members. If that happens, we hold a group meeting to make sure the issue is handled promptly and fairly. And even when it becomes necessary to expel a member (referred to as "weeding") the matter is handled with love and respect.

On a softer note, the level of support many of our Bellas need seems to intensify during the holidays. You see, some members have a very hard time, emotionally, during a traditionally joyous season. The threat and danger of their daily lives makes "joy" a foreign concept.

While others enjoy the closeness of loving families and friends, Christmas drives many inactive Bellas to us for counseling. They know they can count on us to help them get through those very difficult times. Sad to say, but my warriors and I have all been there and sometimes we still are, so it is a wonderful feeling to be able to guide these special ladies over the rough spots in the road.

We have Capos (bosses) as they do in the real Mafia. Most of our Capos have been in the organization for a long time, have proved their dedication and loyalty, and have a strong connection with God. If anything happens to me or Bella Czech, the other Capos have to be ready to step right in and keep things running smoothly. La Bella Mafia meetings are generally conducted via e-mail and include everyone who needs to be involved. Under special circumstances, we schedule conference calls that include me, Bella Czech, Security and the Prayer Warriors, or other combinations appropriate for the decision we must make.

When an issue develops, it is first discussed by me

and Czech. Then we talk it over with the next level of Capos to get a consensus of the appropriate way to bring resolution. Next we contact the person who is causing the difficulty and explain what we believe they have done wrong and how it is affecting the other Bellas. There are two disciplinary steps. The first is a warning and probation. If the offender continues her misconduct, we have no choice but to go to the second step and expel this Bella for the welfare of the group.

In certain instances, particularly with younger Bellas, they might be allowed back if they have matured and understand and acknowledge their mistakes. However, we've found that older members, particularly those who have an evil bent, are much less likely to change. Unfortunately, sometimes you just have to accept that as hard as you try, some people are beyond the help we offer. In such cases, expulsion is the only solution.

We have no hard and fast rules for being part of La Bella Mafia, but we do have specific guidelines. On our La Bella Mafia Facebook page we state:

The La Bella Mafia was created by a few women whose idea of a group isn't who can be the biggest, the baddest, or the toughest. It's a group designed for women who have been there to help to inspire other women. Founded nearly eight years ago by Bella Capo and Bella Czech, La Bella Mafia has consistently maintained a reputation of helping women rise above anything through prayer, a phone call and a sharing of resources.

Although the majority of us are Italian females, we hold no prejudice, and welcome all races. Drama is prohibited and will not be allowed in any shape or form. We deal with real life experiences and find that games and drama produce absolutely no positive results. We are here to help and support one another.

A Bella in Need Can Find A Bella Indeed. God Bless you all.

One of the most important things is to ensure that a Bella feels secure in all situations. Men are allowed and welcome, but they must conduct themselves in a respectful fashion. Our members always have a way to contact us if they experience any form of harassment, need to complain about something or have questions.

La Bella Mafia—Women Helping Women Worldwide.

Fortunately, because we have a very broad variety of skills among our members, we have managed to function as a volunteer network to date. This includes everyone from housewives, to nurses, members of the entertainment industry, security specialists, legal minds—you name it, we've got it.

Often our available funds dictate what we can do for any one Bella. We put as much money as we can together and as many of our resources as we can when a Bella is in need. By focusing on each specific situation, and what it will take to help or get them to safety, we work as a team taking it one step at a time. By doing it this way, we have managed to relocate members who are in threatening situations, refer them to counseling agencies for things we can't handle ourselves, help them to create new identities for their protection, and more. And everything we do is on a volunteer basis.

Everyone has a special dream of their own, even if they don't talk about it much. As for me, my dream is to find a way to offer freedom from fear and the opportunity to discover and enjoy the kind of life society calls normal to as many abuse victims as possible. Think of women like Rose, who was so changed by the simple expression of love when she visited me.

You cannot know the importance of that simple word—normal—unless you have walked in our shoes.

* * *

My mother's voice broke into my thoughts. "What did you just say about 'normal,' Bella? You were mumbling." I straightened with a start. "Say?" Then I realized I must have said the last sentence out loud.

Mom smiled, then walked over and sat next to me on the sofa. She patted my hand gently. "You know, for so long my normal was knowing when or where I could get the next fix or pop the next pills and drop back into oblivion. I'm so sorry I wasn't there for you."

I gave her a hug and wiped away the lone tear inching down her cheek. With that simple statement, "I'm so sorry I wasn't there for you," decades of hurt fell away—much of the hurt and resentment I hoped would disappear in its entirety someday. She had never said it just that way before. And although I'd told her so much since we reconciled, I still wondered sometimes if she realized how abandoned I'd felt my whole life.

I could feel the warmth washing over me as I said, "You're here for me now and it means the world to me. I never thought we would ever see this day and I thank God for finally giving me what I hungered for—a real Mom."

"—and you've given me the ability to enjoy my daughter and beautiful grandchildren and great-grandchildren. I hate to say this, Honey, but we're not done yet. Despite all the therapy both of us have had, you and I know deep down there are things we haven't faced. It will be hard, but you have your Bella successes to draw on for strength. It's finally time to get rid of our ghosts."

CHAPTER TWENTY-SEVEN

For the next few days neither of us began the conversation that would lead to bringing up the ghosts Mom alluded to. Maybe it was because we knew once we opened the door it would be next to impossible to close it.

There was a strong possibility that in the process we would say accusatory or very hurtful things. Not to condemn the other, but because it was necessary—the only way to finally clear the air of the specters that hovered nearby. As a counselor and advocate for others in this position, I finally had to force myself to recognize that I was the one who would have to make the first move. If I didn't, this could hang between us for the rest of our lives—a sliver of resentment in the new fabric of the mother-daughter relationship we had woven.

Four days after that first conversation the time was right. My mother was off that day and the kids were at school. We'd have time to talk before they came home. As I made my way toward the sink, where my mother was rinsing dishes, I remember the air in the house suddenly seemed stuffy and my heart beat like it wanted to jump out of my chest. Each tick of the clock in the kitchen sounded like a hammer hitting metal. Everything around me intensified. I tapped her on the shoulder. "It's time, Mom." I'm sure my voice reflected my reluctance to utter those three words.

She turned, panic reflected in her eyes. "Can we wait for an hour or so?"

"No, Mom. Come with me into the living room. I know this is hard, but we have to do what you said. We have to get rid of those ghosts."

I sat on the sofa. She sat on the edge of one of the chairs facing me, wringing her hands in her lap.

I made my voice soft. "Settle back, this is going to take a while." I'd moved into counselor mode and taken charge of what was to come.

"When I was little and used to do all of those awful things to my dolls, hid food in my closet, the way I tried to avoid my brother—why didn't you ever question any of that? Surely you couldn't have thought it was what kids my age did. When Daddy beat my brother, he beat me. Later it became sexual. I was terrified of him, but both of us were victims."

Although she'd managed to lean back into the comfort of the easy chair, she continued to wring her hands. Tears balanced on the rims of her eyes. "I had to shield myself from every emotion, just like you did, later. When one allows oneself to feel, I—well, I don't think you can deal with the Hell that is your life. It wasn't that I didn't love you or notice. I just couldn't allow myself to react or even acknowledge what I saw. It was easier to pretend deep inside that it wasn't real—an effect of the drugs—lots of them. If I had faced reality, I probably would have gone off the deep end sooner than I did. I'm so sorry."

"I felt like no one was there to protect me. I acted out the life I saw in front of me—abuse, evil. Hell, Mom, I was only four years old with no one to turn to. So, I fantasized that the Devil would take me and it would all be over.

But he didn't, and it wasn't. I heard God telling me I would survive."

A faraway look washed over my mother's face. "I guess somehow I managed to block out all of that. Instead, when I was sober I took you to dancing lessons and made beautiful costumes. I tried to give you something pretty. Something to make my little girl happy. It wasn't enough. I know that now."

"No, it wasn't. But hearing you say that helps me get past it. I guess you were so screwed up yourself, so beaten down by Daddy, there really wasn't a way for you to help me back then. I know I became a handful to manage as I grew older. You were away from me so much. How did you feel when Daddy battered me so badly the time you were in rehab?"

She got up from her chair and sat next to me on the sofa. She put her arms around me and clung to me as she cried softly against my hair.

"Oh, Bella, seeing you with those bruises tore my heart out. I guess it was the first time I really faced what was happening, probably because I was sober. I knew I had to get you away from him and I wasn't at a point where I could take care of you, myself. That's why I took you to the police. I really tried to do what was right. You have to believe me."

I nodded. "Yeah, I do know that. It just didn't turn out right, that's all. Everyone thought Team House was such a good, upstanding organization helping kids with problems. That was just the picture they presented on the outside, while they were brainwashing us. Kids like me were a prime target, but I was too smart for them."

A smile broke across her face. "You sure were, Honey. They fooled all of us, even Ali, but they sure didn't fool you. When I got that call from you it moved me to finally take charge. I had to protect my daughter."

"It was a first step, Mom. I guess that's when I began

to believe that you did love me."

She went back to the chair and leaned forward placing her elbows on her knees. "I know a lot of this was my fault, but you sure weren't easy. I kept telling myself I could deal with whatever you threw my way, but some of it really was beyond me. I guess those were the times I let you down, but you've let me down, too. Still, I guess good comes from bad sometimes, but it sure is hard while it's happening."

At first I bristled when she said I'd let her down. Somehow, in my mind this was all going to be about her failures. Snapping back into counselor mode, I realized that it had been a two-way street and if we were to heal completely, I had to be honest with myself. She had been in a fragile state when I'd come back to live with her shortly after she was out of rehab. My wild streak might have been easier for someone else to control, someone who wasn't wrestling with her own demons, but I'd never let myself acknowledge that.

This time it was my turn to walk over to her and hug her. "I know Mom. Some of the things I did could have sent you back to doing drugs, but you did your best to be there for me and try to guide me. I was too strong for you at times, and that wasn't your fault. I think we've explored enough for today." I glanced at my watch. "And the kids will be home soon."

The healing had begun.

CHAPTER TWENTY-EIGHT

It would have been wonderful if everything fell into place for Mom and me after our first session like it does in the movies or on TV. Unfortunately, life just isn't like that. We were determined to finish what we'd started, though. I questioned whether we were doing the right thing, but in my heart I knew we were, so while the kids were in school, some days were filled with stories or confessions that made us smile or cry. On others we got into shouting matches.

When we came to the part where we talked about Angelo, it became particularly painful. You see, I'd told Mom quite a bit during that time, but not all of it. She really didn't know how deeply involved I became with the Crips, or that in many ways they were responsible for saving my life and those of my children. During that period of time I was in such survival mode I did lots of things automatically. Mom aptly pointed out that had I been able to take the time to really think through the risks I took, I would have realized they probably put not only me, but the kids in danger.

We opened up with each other for several weeks until at last I told her how scared I was when Angelo continued to stalk me.

She sat there shaking her head from side to side, wringing her hands. "Oh, Bella, you should have said something. I'm not sure what I could have done, but—"

"Forget it, Mom. There was nothing you could do about my frustration with the police. I had the damn evidence and the cops wouldn't do anything. You know, I screamed at them that, domestic dispute or not, they were the police. I wanted them to believe that it was so much more than domestic differences. I'd yell, 'He's dangerous. You have to protect me.' But they didn't protect me—the Crips did."

We'd never really talked this frankly before and I have to admit it was overwhelming. I hoped I could go on. My head was spinning and I felt the beginning of a headache.

"You have to understand. I didn't want to get you involved. He was so crazy by then I figured he would go after you, too. It was enough that he didn't care about the kids and had done so many horrible things while we'd been married—things I wouldn't have believed in my wildest dreams. Mom, he was my perfect husband and he turned into a perfect monster right before my eyes. I couldn't put you in that kind of danger."

"But, Bella, if I'd known about the times you didn't have food and the threats you were getting—."

"Actually, I did tell you about some of them. At least I think I did, but because of my dementia and PTSD, so much of that period of time is a blur. At times I wasn't sure some of the things really happened, but when I see concrete evidence in front of me I know they did."

At that point I realized my mother was looking at me with pain in her eyes. Then it registered. Of course. She had gone through the same thing. The disbelief followed by the proof.

I said, "All I know is I went through life one day at a time, kept my 'gangsta girl' attitude and then went to church at night and laid down on the floor crying my eyes out where no one could see my weaknesses. My prayers mixed with my tears. Sure, I went through some really bad stuff, like being raped, and always having to be on guard, but while I was considered to be a boss in the Crips, the truth is they were my protectors. They were the strength against Angelo, and the FBI's abuse."

"But—"

"Shhh, Mom. Trust me, there really wasn't a lot you could have done at that time even if you'd known about it. Besides, in my screwed-up mind I was afraid if I laid much of it on you, you'd try to find an escape in drugs again. I couldn't have that on my head, too."

Righteous determination lit her eyes. "Bella, I've managed to keep sober all of these years. I'm not about to slide now, nor was I then. Maybe I couldn't make things easier for you back then, but I can now. You know I'll help with the girls. They've been through a lot, too, and I see the problems they have. Don't hesitate to lean on me. I'm stronger than you think."

That was one of the good sessions. We got past a lot that day. Her guilt. My guilt. All of it out on the table.

Other days were almost a complete reversal. We would start calmly talking, then escalate into a shouting match—repressed anger rearing its ugly head. Insults and accusations would fly from both sides. Somehow we always followed it with hugs and "I love you," though.

Meanwhile, the number of Bellas was steadily growing. What had been a page on My Space had burgeoned into a formidable organization that was helping me fulfill my promise to God.

***

One day when Mom and I were in our living room having another of our talks, I decided the mood was right for me to tell her something that was on my mind. But it wasn't about the past, it was about the future. "Mom, Tony Nap sent me an email a couple of weeks ago. He said that as close as we are in our relationship, it's time that we met in person."

She broke into a smile. "He's right. With all that man has done for you personally, and the help he has given some of the other Bellas, I think of him as part of our family. Is he coming here?"

"No. He wants me to come to New York so he can show me around."

"When?" was her response, but I sensed her initial enthusiasm had been replaced with concern.

I smiled reassuringly. "You don't have to worry, Mom. I'm not going to leave you and the girls and take off for the Big Apple any time soon. When you and I agree the time is right I'll do it, and not before. When I do go, you won't have to fret about my safety. I trust Tony with my life. I'll be in good hands with him, just like Allstate."

Her smile returned. "Of course you will, Honey. Talking about Tony reminds me, have you spoken with Tracy lately?"

Tracy is Tony's younger half-sister. Their father was Jimmy "Nap" Napoli, a highly respected made man and Capo in New York's Genovese crime family. From the 1950's into the '80s he controlled one of the largest illegal gambling operations in the United States. At one point it was estimated that his organization employed over 2,000 people and grossed $150 million annually. Jimmy maintained ties to most of the major organized crime families and was heavily involved in the Mob's financial interests in Las Vegas.

"Yes, just yesterday," I answered.

"And?"

"She's doing okay, Mom. She's going to be fine."

When our talk ended and Mom headed for the kitchen, I stayed on the sofa and thought about Tracy and Tony.

They are two people I think the world of, yet they haven't seen each other, or even spoken, in years. I met Tracy a couple of years ago when Tony called me and asked if I'd do him a favor. He said his half-sister had dropped out of sight several years earlier and he had just located her in a city not too far from where I live. Would I go see her and make sure she was okay?

I told him I'd be happy to, but wondered if he planned to fly out to see her later, himself or if he had any message he wanted me to give to her. He said he had no message, and went on to explain to me that he had fought his own devils—in this case, booze. Tony was an alcoholic.

He said that as a young man and son of a powerful mobster, he had lived a life very different than most. He adored his father and took to the same lifestyle. Although Jimmy Nap was known as a "gentleman's, gentleman," Tony grew up as a fighter. He fought inside the ring while in the Air Force, and in streets and alleys as part of his chosen career path. He also developed a fierce loyalty, not only to his father, but to all those in "the life."

Jimmy didn't want his son to become a made man—he knew that made men were being increasingly targeted by law enforcement and sent to prison. So Tony functioned as an associate, taking part in certain family activities, but—Jimmy hoped—keeping a low enough profile to stay out of legal trouble.

Unfortunately, living the Mob lifestyle brought Tony face-to-face with many temptations, including a lot of partying. And that's when he met one foe that got the best of him—and it came in a bottle.

The last time he'd seen Tracy there had been an altercation between them. She disappeared shortly afterward. Not knowing if she was dead or alive, he looked for her on and off during the nearly two decades since their last contact. He finally located her in a medical facility in my new home state, suffering from severe PTSD. He doubted she knew he'd turned his life around and had been sober for 17 years, or that to atone for his harmful actions in the past, he is doing volunteer work helping military veterans with service-connected injuries receive the benefits they are entitled to. Under the circumstances, he felt it would be better that he not just show up or send word that could further upset her. It was certainly a sad story and I couldn't argue with Tony's logic. A few days later I walked into the hospital and met Tracy.

Tony's information had been accurate, her PTSD was severe. I told her that Tony wasn't trying to get back into her life, that he was simply concerned about her and had asked me to look in on her and see if she needed anything. After that initial explanation, we didn't talk about Tony for the rest of the day. Instead, I wanted to make her my friend—someone she could trust and confide in. There would be time enough to fill her in on Tony, afterward.

In the intervening months, Tracy and I became very close. She is an absolute sweetheart and I visit her in person whenever possible and talk with her by phone in the interim. My mother has never met her in person, yet she feels the same way about her that I do.

I have updated Tracy on her brother a little at a time, not wanting to make her feel pushed or threatened. She's gradually coming to realize that the Tony of today is not the same man he was all those years ago. But she is still reluctant to rekindle their relationship.

I keep Tony posted on her condition and her attitude toward him. To his credit, he understands this is a slow process and is very patient. He sends me money every so often to buy her anything she needs, but never asks me to pressure her when it comes to her feelings about him.

Tracy is now willing to accept a photo of Tony to hang in her room. That may not sound like much, but I think it's a major step. My goal is to see them meet again in person and let bygones be bygones. I know that would be good for both of them. And with God's help it will happen.

CHAPTER TWENTY-NINE

Tony Nap wasn't the only one who urged me to write a book. I'd tucked most of my memories away in a safe place deep down inside me where even I couldn't reach all of them, but for years many of the people I came in contact with said the same thing, "You have to write a book." It seems strange now, but for some reason I can't recall ever taking them seriously—that is until a couple of years ago.

That is when I acknowledged that if I wrote my book it would have the power to help others like me. Women who suffer but don't know who to reach out to—and maybe it would also put my own demons to rest. I knew one thing for sure—although I'm a good writer, I would need help. There was so much material and I was too close to it. I would have to consult with someone to sort through everything, to figure out what to include and what to discard and, most importantly, to produce a proper manuscript. One of my friends knew a professional writer, so I agreed to talk to him.

It didn't go well, and at one point I thought about giving up the idea of writing a book. He was impossible to convince that I had survived so many unusual experiences in my relatively short life. There is more than ample proof that these things happened, but he was blindsided by his condescending attitude and disbelief. I thanked my friend for hooking us up, then said I didn't think it was going to work out. After that, nothing more was said about a book for a few months. Oh, I'd jot down notes here and there, stuff them in a file and tell myself I'd make it happen one day, but often just the act of putting some of it on paper was enough to throw me into depression sometimes for as long as a week.

A few months later, another friend asked how the book was coming.

I told her, "I'm afraid it isn't happening. I spoke to a writer who wanted to help me put it together, but we definitely didn't click." This did not deter her, and she answered, "Well, I wasn't going to say anything, but you know my cousin has written some pretty explosive books. Do you want me to feel him out and see if he's interested?"

At first I was going to say "no", but then I reconsidered. Maybe her cousin would be "the one" and I didn't want to blow it. "Okay, ask him to email me. I'm not sure I want to give out my phone number until I test the water, so to speak."

This fellow turned out to be an investigative reporter and my antennae went up immediately. Even in the initial email he asked me a lot of questions that smacked of his desire to sensationalize everything. I sincerely doubted his ability to hold certain information confidential, and that was imperative. I was in hiding and afraid for my life at times. I certainly wasn't going to give him the key to where I was without actually knowing or meeting him, and I certainly wasn't going to get in bed with someone whose desire for personal success would exploit what I told him and put me in jeopardy.

My answer to him was short. Something like, "Thanks for your interest but I think we have different objectives. I wish you luck on your other projects."

Once again I was ready to forget it.

Then one of my best friends, Bella Bling, who calls herself "Italians Do It Better," kept after me to not drop the book idea, but to continue looking for the right person to collaborate with. Bella Bling and I have shared many experiences and she understands where we are and where we've been. That is why when I read the following post from her, it meant so much to me. She is very funny and very smart, too. We spent many days and nights together, either online or on the telephone. An amazing woman, she has also has been through her own Hell, like all of us.

Over many months, we dredged up memories and experiences from each of our pasts. Things we had repressed because we were unwilling or unable to face them. Bella was there to comfort my many tears.

Bella Bling's post:

Bella Capo is an amazing and wonderful woman with a heart of gold. Her strength and self-determination are astonishing to me. She exists as an inspiration for people to "Fight Back." From the love of her family and her unwavering faith she survived lurid and shocking battles that I am amazed to hear about. She's a true Bella.

My heart goes out to her and I cherish our friendship and her creative insight, advice, and sense of humor. Through God, prayer, determination, and pure will power she musters up the strength to be able to tell the nightmares that were her reality. Bella Capo won my heart and my trust (which isn't easy) by being one of the most honest and caring people I ever met.

She has been through so much heart-breaking pain, I wish I could take it away. As I learned more about her through her stories, not just her stories but her life, I saw that her faith in God and her children helped her survive. Bella's innocent heart just wanted love and a home so desperately. Instead, so much happened that hurt her physically, mentally, and emotionally, but not spiritually. Some people have one or two major events in their life, but she has enough for fifty people.

Her goal has always been to help women. To show them an enthusiastic and free spirit that can be had even from someone who shouldn't even be alive with all that she has encountered. She supports all of her Bella's in "La Bella Mafia" by encouraging them to be strong through their trials and errors, even when she is fighting so many battles herself. Ours is A Mafia of Love.

She gives you a shoulder to cry on or a slap if you're out of line! LOL! She does tell it like it is! I value her wit, street smarts, intelligence, and sarcasm and we laugh for hours! I enjoy her free spirit and her laugh is absolutely hilarious! My heart broke for her, as I witnessed the tears and sobbing when she spoke about her life and then I would be amazed and still am, at how well she recovered and bounced right back to her spunky self.

To write a book and have to relive the stories again is astonishing. She is inspirational because her heart is so big and she wears it on her sleeve. She is compassionate, caring, funny, silly, and a very strong woman and mother who cherishes her family and friends and is soooo loved by me.

She is proud of her Italian heritage, loyal, sassy, and a woman of integrity, resilience, and a fabulous best friend. Even when she talked about writing her book, after spilling her heart to me through the tears, she always thought of me. Despite all she goes through, she always has time or makes time to help me or just to talk to me and I love her for that. I know it's a friendship and trust that will last a lifetime.

Most important, she proved to me that if you stand your ground and never lose sight of your dreams, they can come true. When she writes La Bella Mafia it will be with her tears...tears of anger, fear, sadness, but also tears of joy so that her story can help other women. There isn't a selfish bone in her body to be thinking like that and she's lov-

able like a teddy bear. I want to protect her and love her so she never has to feel pain again. She is bellalicious! A true Bella because she is a fighter...and she has been fighting back throughout her life.

Wow! What can you say after reading something like that? Certainly not, "I give up. I'm not going to do it." That would be contrary to everything I try to impart to my Bellas.

The post from Bella Bling wasn't unusual. Many of the Bellas write notes about me, maybe not as long as that one, but with similar messages.

After a number of false starts with writers, I turned to Tony Nap. I never really wanted to go to him for help with the book because he had done so much for me already, and I didn't want to impose on our friendship. But it was becoming crunch time. I knew he'd written a book about his life and no one understands me better than Tony, so I reached out to him and explained I was trying to find a writer I would be comfortable working with. I knew he would know what I needed from a writer and I trusted him to find that person for me. Rather than treating my plea for help as an imposition, he was ecstatic.

"Good. You finally listened to me and you're gonna do it."

I didn't have the heart to tell him I'd spoken to other writers before mentioning it to him.

He continued like a proud father, "Okay, I got just the guy for you, name of Dennis Griffin. He's helped to write books for some former mob guys and has a real talent for dealing with true crime and true stories. Do you want to talk to him?"

I had to know one thing first, but being it was Tony I should have known it went without saying. "Can I trust him? That's really important, Tony."

He chuckled. "Like a brother."

Denny and I clicked instantly and we began to trade

emails about what I wanted to accomplish. Then I received a call from him one day. "There is a woman I know who I'd like to bring into the project if it's okay with you. Her name is Morgan St. James and she's good. One of her books deals with a young girl who was kidnapped and raped, then left for dead. It's fiction, but I think you'll relate to it."

"Do you think she'll be interested?"

"Why don't I send her your bullet points and see?"

Well, he did and she was. During the process I discovered she'd had PTSD from an auto accident several years before and related completely to some of the things I deal with daily. That was really important, because sometimes PTSD makes you feel like you're crazy. I had a good feeling about everything and all that was left was to start writing.

By going to Tony I didn't just get a writer—I got a team.

CHAPTER THIRTY

In April of 2013 I got to meet Denny and Morgan in person. For nearly a year we'd been writing this book via emails, telephone and Skype. Now the big day had finally arrived. I was going to Las Vegas to sign the contract, meet my publisher and, most of all, meet the two people I'd come to think of as family.

It was a little frightening, because this would be the first time in a long time I was traveling by myself. You see, although "the package" looks good on the outside, no one who sees me or meets me would ever think I have the daily challenges of PTSD, Traumatic Brain Injury and dementia. But I do. This was a big step and I was ready.

Houdini Publishing had a large event arranged to introduce their authors to the media, and although it was hard to believe, I was included. This was one of the last steps in my book becoming a reality. Denny met me at the airport and I gave him hugs like no tomorrow.

When I met Morgan and stayed at her house, it was like I'd come into the womb of family. The day of the event, Morgan helped me pick out my outfit and suggested how to arrange my hair. When we were done she said I looked like a Grecian Goddess, and to my enormous surprise, I felt like one.

The event was amazing. I was the old Bella, working the crowd, talking to everyone I could. My PTSD was on hold and I was back in the groove. The authors were invited one-by-one to come up to the microphone and address the audience.

Denny was called up after several authors. He talked about his other books, and then asked Morgan to join him at the mic. I sat there watching, so happy to be alive. Denny sat down, and Morgan told the audience a little about her writing background and how she had come into the *La Bella Mafia* project. Then, to my shock and surprise, Morgan said, "Bella Capo is with us tonight, and I'd like to introduce her to all of you. Please, Bella, come up and say a few words."

My heart began to pound like a kettle drum and when I looked at my hands, they were shaking. Me, the one who used to get up in front of crowds sometimes numbering in the thousands. Why was I shaking like a leaf?

In my head I heard, "You have to do this. You can do this." Whether it was God or my inner angel speaking to me, the message was clear. I grabbed my half-glass of champagne, downed it in nearly one gulp, squared my shoulders and faced my fear.

Once I held the mic, I didn't even have to think about what I was going to say because the words began to flow magically. Morgan sat down and left me there. I spoke a bit about things I'd survived in my life, my love of God. There wasn't a sound from the audience and I thought I was doing pretty well. Everyone seemed to be hanging on my words.

Then the PTSD kicked in and the tears welled in my eyes. No! I couldn't break down now. I had to keep going. But I couldn't hold them back, and suddenly Morgan was there at my side to catch me, saying on her way up, "Mama Bella Morgan to the rescue," then she gave me hugs and rubbed my back. I realized that she was unconsciously rubbing the spot where my crying angel is tattooed. That's right. No more crying angels, because I'm able to cry for myself now. But I was determined not to shed the tears then.

I regained my composure and looked out at the audience, surprised to see that many of them were wiping tears from their own eyes. Morgan left me on my own again.

Afterwards, people lined up at our table to talk to me, and I knew my dream was about to come true. Soon I would hold a copy of *La Bella Mafia* in my hand and do everything possible for my story, my book, to help others who were enduring or had endured experiences similar to mine.

AFTERWORD

When I met Bella in person for the first time, there was an instant connection. I felt as though I was welcoming a daughter back home. We'd all been through a lot during the journey of writing *La Bella Mafia*—Bella, Denny, Judy and me—so although we had never physically met, Bella and I knew each other intimately in our hearts. We had shared stories, laughter and yes, many tears.

It has been mentioned that I had PTSD from a life-threatening accident years before, so I thoroughly understand things that Bella goes through every day of her life. Mine was mild and hers is severe, but the feelings are the same. Mine is just about gone, hers lingers like an uninvited guest who has overstayed its welcome.

It is a strange affliction, and someone who has not walked in our shoes might think the symptoms are over-dramatized—sudden bouts of tears, blank spots in our memory, possibly overacting to events—but trust me, it is all real and even with counseling, there are some aspects of it that never go away. For years, if I heard the brakes on a car screeching, there would be a humming in my head and the sensation of being in a whirlpool, reminiscent of all of the spins my car took after being hit.

So, although I saw so many strengths in our Bella, I also instinctively knew her weaknesses and during our visit was always ready to give her support without hesitation, question or qualification. She is an extremely strong and positive woman, but those little chinks in her armor allow the demons to sneak in sometimes. We also share various experiences in common that furthered the bond between us, but I won't go into that. This is her book, not mine.

What I was able to witness during her stay with me was how dedicated she is to her Bellas and her intense commitment to do everything possible for others in need, even when she is in pain or facing other challenges herself. This is a woman whose involvement never stops. From the moment she awakens in the morning, sometimes even before she's been able to have as much as a cup of coffee, she is on the La Bella Mafia website or Facebook page, checking to see who needs help. She told me even when her PTSD would not allow her to get out of bed or off the couch, the laptop was perched on her stomach so she could manage and organize anything and everything that needed to be done to help a Bella.

It was obvious to me she spends most of her days on the computer and on the phone counseling women in jeopardy and helping them to escape bad situations, deal with kidnappings, abuse and more. I witnessed what a loving and guiding soul she is with these needy people. At times, after a call, she would break down and cry for other things in her own life, and I'd hug her and bring her back. That is so common with PTSD, as I unfortunately know from experience.

It seems it never stops and she and the other main Bellas are there just about 24/7, offering counseling, support and solutions. There are so many telephone calls, I kidded her that she needed an implanted cell phone. The calls come in one after another and I said she is bound to get a sore neck from cradling the phone between her neck and shoulder for hours on end.

Every situation, whether life-threatening or less critical, is handled in her smooth, soft, comforting voice. She analyzes what is needed and takes any necessary action or delegates to another Bella who is best qualified to handle a particular situation. The posts and calls aren't all bad news, either. There are the successes, those women and some men, who have navigated from the gloom into the sunshine with the help of La Bella Mafia.

Although the phone rings constantly—in the car, in a restaurant, while watching TV—wherever she is or whatever she is doing, the call is answered.

I am sure many of those calls affect her dramatically because they dredge up her own memories and all of the abuses she suffered throughout her life. You simply can't smash down everything, particularly after the lid has been lifted. When I saw Bella Capo's shoulders shake at the podium and her eyes fill with tears, I ached for what it must take out of her to help others. Mama Bella, as she calls me, jumped into action and gave her needed hugs. I'm sure she is by herself many times when this crying and shaking takes over. I was happy to be able to talk about the good work she was doing while I comforted her. My heart filled with love and pride to know someone like her who puts the needs of others before her own.

We in Team Bella are all honorary "Bellas" now, and our contribution has been to take this collection of lifelong stories that cover every emotion and situation from tragedy to triumph, and craft them into a book that doesn't sugarcoat anything. It is a story that needed to be told, and we are beyond complimented to be the people who were chosen to be trusted with unvarnished details. Before you ask, yes, backup of what you have read in this true account of Bella's life has been provided to us—this is, indeed, a woman who should have died many times, but endures.

Bella Capo is a loving, caring mother to her own children and the extended family that includes hundreds of kindred souls, the heart and soul of La Bella Mafia.

Thank you for taking the time to read her story. It is a life most of us can never imagine and therefore it holds what is called a morbid fascination. We who have led sheltered lives are given a peek at what could have been us but for the grace of God. For the women or men who read this and recognize snippets from their own lives, I hope we have provided the inspiration to know that by facing the demons and seeking help, you can find the path to a better life.

Morgan St. James
Las Vegas, NV
April 2013

EPILOGUE

And so, my readers, as we reach the end of this story, we begin a new chapter in my life. You have journeyed with me through my past, and understand my commitment to finish what I start. Now I want to share my vision of what I hope the future holds. This book will go a long way toward helping me to achieve my goals, but there is more to be done.

La Bella Mafia, the online organization, currently has hundreds of members. However, every day I ask myself how I can reach others who have either entered shelters or are suffering in silence.

When you are being sucked into the mire of what your life has become, it is very hard to be positive—to believe that you are entitled to a life most people consider ordinary. Because this book has helped me to unearth incidents and feelings that even the therapists were not able to reach, and gave me the ability to verbalize them, I rediscovered what I'd really always known. Those who are downtrodden as a result of threatening or horrific experiences will listen to, but not take direction from, a speaker or counselor who has never endured physical and mental abuse. Instead, they may think something akin to, "Sure, that's easy for them to say. What if they were really in my situation?"

College classes and studies for advanced degrees go a long way in teaching a counselor or therapist how to communicate and offer resolutions. But as a survivor, I can look people in the eye while I relate my own experiences to theirs and offer real time suggestions and possible solutions, thereby gaining their trust and commitment. They understand that I suffer along with them and the advice I put forward comes from the heart and firsthand experience, not textbooks. And it works in the scheme of real life.

So now I must find a way to reach out to abused women's help organizations across the nation, tell my story and offer the gift of hope. Obviously, the number of people I would like to reach would not have been possible from a cost or time aspect years ago. But in this digital age, something like this is not only far easier than it would have been, but is entirely possible. While I can't travel to every safe house and organization in the country, I can make and distribute instructional videos and contribute copies of my book. These materials could be shared among a multitude of individuals, groups, and interested and affected parties.

Although I now consider myself to be hiding in plain sight, I still have to be somewhat guarded about my visibility, so I don't envision this as being a commercial venture with the video orderable or openly online. Instead, the book and video would be distributed to legitimate organizations identified by my team. These materials and my new blog will provide encouragement, inspiration and guidance.

Much like the Stockholm Syndrome seen in prisoners of war, women in life-threatening situations involving physical or mental abuse, identify with their abusers and may try to protect and/or return to these people. My greatest hope is to have some small part in the urgent action required to make them understand that they must remain removed from their current conditions and not look back. The alternative can be death by murder or suicide.

The La Bella Mafia group has occasionally offered assistance in relocating and creating a new identity for Bellas in jeopardy which makes it extremely difficult for their abuser to find them. While some of the elements of rescue can be costly, we are fiscally conservative and utilize volunteers— including myself and other Bellas. We negotiate discounts for additional services and products, and also hope to attract sponsors.

In closing, if I've ever given you the impression that I

think this will be a piece of cake, I didn't mean to. I know it will take a massive commitment in time and effort by me and others. But I believe in the old saying, "Where there's a will, there's a way." And it must be obvious to you by now that I believe in my cause. The words "give up" are no longer a part of my vocabulary.

God has steered me in the right direction, and I have no doubt that He will do so in this case, as well. He didn't bring me safely through all of my own trials and tribulations, and sustain me through the traumatic experience of writing this book, only to stop within sight of my next goal. I made a vow to Him and I won't rest until I deliver on it. And that's a promise you can take to the bank!

* * *

There is one more thing I want to share with you—the lyrics I wrote that morning as the sun was rising over Sunset Strip. I held them close to my heart for about fifteen years as I learned how to cry. During that time, many producers approached me about putting *No More Crying Angels* to music and recording it, but somehow I never felt the time was quite right. You see, because I was pouring out my soul in those words, as I wrote I experienced emotions that had been smashed down for many years. I was the lyrics and they were me. To give my words to someone else, everything had to be exactly right from the music to the singer and producer. It will be on the air someday—that I know. But for now, here is *No More Crying Angels©*.

For legal reasons, I do need to tell you that it is protected by my copyright. If you wish to use *No More Crying Angels©* in any way, please contact me through my publisher for my permission.

NO MORE CRYING ANGELS©

This fear you've found inside my soul
How could anyone understand?
Pain and politics
The truth of my life
Reality
To only me.

I've never believed in what I've heard
It's the ears in my heart
Where the lies were not heard

I've never believed
Free me with justice
Subliminal truth
That's here for me now
Through my angels youth.

I hope you see
And understand
It's almost claimed
Is it my man?
Only He will come inside
And heal these wounds
I've had to hide

It's not His fault
He'll already know
That once united
White light will grow.

But I've never believed
In what I've heard
It's the eyes in my heart
where the light was pure

I never believed.
Free me with justice
Subliminal youth

That's here for me now
Through my angels truth.
If it's false or make believe
I'll be the first
He's never deceived
I'm too tired now
To sit and stand
Through politics
And half told plans
My body's death
I do not fear
For all my angels are
Standing near

Maybe God's the only one
Maybe my duties here are done
But if not and here He hides
I'll have no doubt that it's my time

Cause I've never believed
In what I've heard
It's the ears in my heart
Where the lies were not heard

How can I believe
I've never believed
Now I'll go home
Truly knowing
I've made my lessons clear
I'll always stand high
Politically correct
For only the dirty souls
Will lack respect

In this I believe…..

Bella Capo
May 20, 2013

ABOUT THE AUTHORS

Dennis N. Griffin

Dennis N. Griffin retired in 1994, after a 20-year career in investigations and law enforcement in New York State. Shortly afterward he wrote his first novel, *The Morgue*. He currently has seven published mystery/thrillers.

Dennis' debut in nonfiction, *Policing Las Vegas – A History of Law Enforcement in Southern Nevada*, was released in April 2005. It covers the evolution of law enforcement in Las Vegas and Clark County from the City's establishment in 1905. A July 2006 release and Computer Times Editor's Selection three months later, his second nonfiction, *The Battle for Las Vegas – The Law versus the Mob*, tells the story of the Tony Spilotro era in Las Vegas from 1971 through 1986. Dennis' third nonfiction effort, released in July 2007, was *CULLOTTA*, the biography of former Chicago and Las Vegas mobster Frank Cullotta. His latest Mob book is *Surviving The Mob*, the biography of former Gambino crime family associate Andrew DiDionato, which hit store shelves in January 2011.

In October 2012, Dennis' first entertainment-related book, *House Party Tonight*, the story of legendary saxophonist Don Hill, was published by Houdini Publishing. That book was followed in December by *Rogue Town*, the true story of crime and corruption in Stamford, Connecticut, also by Houdini.

Dennis is co-host of the popular Blog Talk Radio show *We Knowa Guy*, and serves as a consultant to the Vegas Mob Tour. He recently opened BEAR Media Consultants, which helps match true crime movie and documentary producers, writers and event coordinators, with potential technical consultants and speakers for their projects or events.

He is an active member of the Wednesday Warrior Writers, Public Safety Writers Association and GLAWS.

Morgan St. James

Award-winning Author/Speaker/Columnist Morgan St. James' most recent books are *Confessions of a Cougar* and *Who's Got the Money*. *Who's Got the Money?* is a fictional funny crime caper inspired by true events experienced by Morgan and her co-author Meredith Holland. It was a finalist in the 2012 USA Book News Best Books Awards. Funny and romantic, *Confessions of a Cougar*, is a creative non-fiction book, the true story of coming of age at 42 with some delicious young guys in England.

After writing magazine and newspaper articles, she launched a career writing fiction with her sister Phyllice Bradner, also a published writer, in the late 1990s. The debut Silver Sisters Mystery, *A Corpse in the Soup*, garnered the USA Book News award as Best Mystery Audio Book 2007. Her list of Silver Sisters Mysteries continued to grow. *A Corpse in the Soup* was followed by *Terror in a Teapot* and *Vanishing Act in Vegas*, the third comical Silver Sisters Mystery. A fourth, *Diamonds in the Dumpster*, is currently in work.

Her short stories appear in *Chicken Soup for the Soul* books and multiple other anthologies. Her recently released single author anthology, *The MAFIA FUNERAL and Other Short Stories*, covers everything from true stories to fiction, mystery to romance and some genres in-between. She has written over 500 published articles relative to the craft of writing and people in the industry, as well as the book *Writers' Tricks of the Trade: 39 Things You Need to Know About the ABCs of Writing Fiction*.

St. James is an entertaining speaker, and frequently appears on radio talk shows, presents workshops and appears on or moderates author's panels. She edits and publishes the online eZine Writers Tricks of the Trade and writes columns for the Los Angeles and Las Vegas editions of Examiner.com.

She is a member of Henderson Writers Group, Las

Vegas Writers Group, Sisters in Crime, GLAWS and PSWA. Visit her websites

www.morganstjames-author.com

http://morgan-james.blogspot.com

http://silversistersmysteries.wordpress.com

http://funnycrimecapers.blogspot.com

http://writerstricksofthetrade.blogspot.com